D1389160

AN INTRODUCTION TO HOLINESS

AN INTRODUCTION TO HOLINESS

BY

HENRI PETITOT, O.P.

Author of
St. Bernadette, St. Thérèse of the Child Jesus, etc.

Translated from the French
by
MALACHY GERARD CARROLL

1950
THE MERCIER PRESS LIMITED
CORK AND LIVERPOOL

Nihil Obstat:

Robert Powell
Censor Deputatus

Imprimatur:

+ Daniel
Episcopus Corcagiensis

die 8 Augusti, 1949

First published by
THE MERCIER PRESS LIMITED
19 Maylor Street, Cork, and
17 Moorfields, Liverpool 2

Made in Great Britain at the Pitman Press

CONTENTS

Essential Preface   I

PART ONE

The Ascetic Life:

1. Primordial Necessity of Asceticism   9
2. Of Humility and the Graces it Wins   25
3. Prayer, Vocal and Mental   43

PART TWO

The Active Life

4. The Apostolic Life   61
5. The Study of Christian Doctrine   77
6. Of Religious Art and its Importance   91

PART THREE

The Unitive Life

7. Necessary and Providential Trials   109
8. The Love of God   125
9. The Love of the Neighbour   140
10. " Many Called, Few Chosen "   155

CONCLUSION

The Mystical Body   170

ESSENTIAL PREFACE

You are the salt of the earth, you are the light of the world.
Our Saviour addressed these prophetic words to his
apostles and to his disciples in general. Taking the
Gospel words strictly, it would seem as though they were
addressed exclusively to men. The Church, in her Liturgy,
notably in the Mass of a Doctor, has applied these words
of Our Saviour to men, and it is an historical fact that
no woman has been made a Doctor of the Church, though
this is not a necessary state of affairs and may, perhaps,
not always be so. The more humanity, Christianized,
progresses, the more the woman sees her influence in
society grow. Even among the Jews, the most religious
of the ancient peoples, the woman, who had so often and
at such different times played an important part in their
history, was scarcely considered.

It remained for Christ to come and place woman in the
first order in Christianity.

It would be superfluous to recall here the sanctifying,
redemptory and reformatory influence exercised by the
woman martyrs among the saints, who shed their blood in
the arena; by those who seconded the Apostles, the
Doctors, the Monks in their evangelization of the people.
With the passage of the centuries, the apostolic role of
saintly Christian women has greatly increased.

The words of Christ: *You are the salt of the earth you are
the light of the world,* apply therefore to both men and

women, and indeed we can say that a number of men and women, called by a vocation or by special graces to the practice of a more perfect Christian life, either in Religion or in the world, must needs be the salt of the earth. When, in an atmosphere of religion and piety, a person begins to lament the evils of the time, the ever growing infidelity and impiety, does he not often forget to ask himself if, when he has been called to be the salt of the earth, he is too easily content with mediocre Christian virtue? The world would certainly not be so corrupt, if all those who have received education and sufficient grace for self-sanctification, fulfilled perfectly what can be truly called their mission.

We do not examine ourselves sufficiently in this matter. The obligations which result from the graces which have been heaped upon us, can be the cause, if we are negligent, of more serious sins than we would consider possible. In a chapter of her *Visions* entitled *the Menace*, Angela de Foligno speaks severely on this subject: " Those who have the Lord God for Instructor, but do not wish to listen to the voice of Him Who speaks in the soul, preferring to turn from it to the voice of common things, such as these shall be cursed by Almighty God." Those who are astonished at the hardness of this saying could, with great profit, turn out its context and read her commentary. Without going so far, we yet maintain that infidelity to a high vocation always implied, at least in practice, many venial sins. Moreover, experience and history teach us that persons, called by their gifts of intelligence, of will, of divine favours to lead a more perfect Christian life, cannot be as easily satisfied as others with a life of honest mediocrity. Because they do not reach up towards the heights, they fall into the depths of unbelief, and become the prey of their own pride and passions.

In considering such examples, souls who feel themselves capable, with the grace of God, of a higher perfection, will be led to make salutary reflexions on the responsibility and the perils they incur, if they remain in a rut of mediocrity.

We have called this book *A Spiritual Renaissance*, the generic title which we have given to our work on St. Thérèse of Lisieux; because in this book, we find constant inspiration in her life and in her doctrine. We have already said, and of this we have become more and more convinced, that there is not a phrase of her writing nor an incident of her life, which has not been providentially destined to serve as a lesson and an example to our age. We also follow St. Teresa of Avila, St. John of the Cross and many other saints. However, as we are strictly Thomists, everything that we advance will be, unless we are very mistaken, legitimate and confirmed by the *Summa* of St. Thomas. We admit that certain Catholics can sit down at the feet of other theologians, but we fail to see how they can add anything essential to Christian doctrine which is not contained, at least virtually, in the *Summa*.

As to the method we follow, we did not bind ourselves to a rigorous plan. Consequently, a reader who is formed to a more logical discipline, may sometimes be disconcerted by unexpected digressions, or by developments of thought which seem repetitions or, a more serious matter, apparent contradictions of developments elsewhere. But, if one overlooks the imperfections of details which prevent him from viewing the work as a whole, he will realise that the method followed here is the *method of the heart— l'ordre du coeur*. This is the method which guided the composition of the *Holy Lives*, the *Imitation* and the principal works of the great mystics.

As to the contradictions which apparently irreconcilable

passages seem to present, we could answer with a comparison of Bossuet's which is often cited: one must hold, in spiritual things, both ends of the chain, in order that one may see clearly all the links by which they are joined; but we prefer to justify ourselves by quoting a *pensée* of Pascal, less known but more significant: " There are a great number of truths, both of faith and morals, in the Church, which seem contradictory, and yet stand side by side in a beautiful order." Only, in order that this *beautiful order* may be appreciated, we must consider all truths, as Pascal says, together and in a single glance.

It must also be noticed that we are not concerned precisely, in this book, with beginners. Though we treat in the beginning, of the ascetic life and of those daily sacrifices which cannot be neglected even by the greatest saints, we have had in mind those souls who have already had some experience in the ways of perfection. It is to all pious persons, who sincerely desire to make progress in holiness, and to Religious, that we dedicate this work, which makes no pretence to being a didactic and complete treatise of the spiritual life. If we use the sub-title, *An Introduction to Holiness*, it is simply to indicate that we aim at leading generous souls to the threshold of perfection, and leave to more competent guides to introduce them into its sanctuary.

We have felt the constant need of being of service, to the best of our ability, to those souls who give themselves at one and the same time to the apostolate and to the interior life. This preoccupation results from our essential design of contributing to a spiritual renaissance. It is useless to keep repeating that there is, in our day, a renewal of the interior life among Catholics. The master idea which has guided us in this work, is the defining of the most necessary conditions for the growth of this renewal. This idea must not be forgotten, because it explains many apparently superfluous digressions, both when we treat of individual holiness and the holiness essential to a group. We constantly consider the bearing of this perfection or of this holiness on the general well-being of humanity. St. Thérèse of the Infant Jesus is still our model in this, through the spirituality she has expressed in her writings and in her life. However, if we do not address ourselves precisely to purely contemplative souls, we yet make this important remark: no contemplative should neglect, at least in prayer and sacrifice, the apostolic character without which there can be no true Christian life.

By avoiding deliberately all theological and technical expressions, this book is made palatable to a greater number of people, and we prayerfully hope that it may be so. If only a few pages prove useful to souls of good will, we are amply rewarded for the pains we have taken.

We beg St. Thérèse of the Child Jesus to bless this little work, inspired, we have no doubt, by her doctrine and by the example of her life. We beg her to obtain for its readers the strength and all the graces necessary to practise the precepts and the salutary counsels which it may contain, and which we judge to be in complete conformity with the traditional teaching of the Church.

Part One

THE ASCETIC LIFE

Chapter One

THE PRIMORDIAL NECESSITY OF ASCETICISM

St. thérèse, at the age of fourteen explained to her sister, Céline, why she chose to enter Carmel, in spite of a burning desire to be a missionary and a strong inclination to join a Foreign Missions Society. " It was," she said, " in order that I should suffer more, and thereby gain more souls for Jesus." The work of conquering oneself is, in her opinion, the most toilsome of all.

Whatever the vocation chosen—be it the contemplative life, the active life, or that life which must be a mixture of both—this toilsome struggle to overcome and to conquer oneself must attend the very first steps in the religious life, and must continue along the entire way, at least against certain faults. This is the sense of Bossuet's words: " We must fight even unto death against the evil we contracted in birth." With equal emphasis, P. Gardeil writes in *La structure de l'âme et l'expérience mystique*: " Whatsoever the aberrations of our conduct or the lowering of our ideals, the war of the spirit against the flesh must remain the great human concern."

A great number of Scriptural texts could be marshalled in support of this truth. " The life of man upon earth is a warfare," says Job; and the book of Proberbs has: " He that ruleth himself is greater than he that taketh a city." The Old Testament harps constantly on the idea of a civil war in the virtuous man—spirit against flesh: but it is St. Paul who does so mostly eloquently. " We know that the law is spiritual, but I am carnal, born under the law of sin. . . . I do not that which I wish, but the evil that I hate, that I do. . . . For I know that in me (that is, in my flesh) dwelleth no good thing. . . . According to the interior man, I delight in the law of God. But I find in my members another law, fighting against the law of my spirit and holding me captive in habits of sin. Unhappy man that I am, who will deliver me from the body of this death? " (Rom. VII.) It is because he has experienced the fierceness and tenacity of human passions that St. Paul can cry out in such distress. He writes to the Corinthians: " You know well enough that when men run in a race, the race is for all, but the prize for one; run, then, for victory. Every athlete must keep all his appetites under control; and he does it to win a crown that fades, whereas ours is imperishable. So I do not run my course like a man in doubt of his goal; I do not fight my battle like a man who wastes his blows on the air. I buffet my own body, and make it my slave; or I, who have preached to others, may myself be rejected as worthless." (Cor. IX.)

This quotation from an Apostle who was a vessel of election and who knew what it was to be rapt into the seventh heaven, will suffice to prove the constant necessity of mortification both of soul and body.

We pass on to a truth which, though we state it briefly here, is of capital importance. Theoretically, the idea of mortification can be analysed, and categories named— physical, intellectual, moral—and this, of course, is quite legitimate; but things distinct in theory often resolve themselves, in practice, to a single unity. Thus, the saints and all the blessed who serve as our models, have given themselves to asceticism in all its forms, and have not laid aside all bodily mortification in order to devote themselves exclusively to the mortification of the senses and of the spirit.

Of course, the importance they attached to bodily mortification varied from saint to saint, but they all took good care not to neglect it entirely. The true spirit of mortification extends to the whole human personality, and that is why Christian asceticism must of necessity be both physical and moral. To believe that one can correct imperfections and advance in the way of perfection, without at the same time—and, indeed, as a preliminary —fighting to subject one's appetites, is a dangerous illusion to which we are particularly prone to-day. We persuade ourselves more and more that, both because of our weakened health and the nature of the times in which we live, we are no longer to imitate the frightful penances of the Desert Fathers. We have not forgotten the counsel, given so energetically by the Little Flower: " Believe me, my Mother, we must be on our guard against these macerations: do not let us set our feet in that way, for it is not the way of little souls like ours."

We esteem highly the extraordinary and sensational penances which the Curé of Ars inflicted on himself till death, and we regard them as having been necessary for the converting of a depraved parish, more than for his personal sanctification. That is why we share so completely the opinion of the Abbé Trochu that these penances " are to be admired rather than imitated," but it does not follow that we ought to neglect completely the sacrifices which are often so sore on our self-love and our love of comfort.

St. Thérèse herself has given, during her whole life, examples of the need for such mortification. Sometimes, indeed, she found it advisable, with the permission of her

Director, to take a severe discipline with the object of conquering some moral imperfection. St. Madeleine Barat, a saint of such calm and even disposition that she seemed little inclined to great physical mortification, confided to one of her daughters: " There was a time when I was so troubled with impatience, that there seemed but one remedy. I took the discipline, *I beat myself as severely as I could*, and only thus could I bring calm to my soul. The saint, however, recommends a superior to use great discretion in according permission for such mortification. " I am not nervous," she adds, " and yet, when I used the discipline, such a trembling seized me that I was unable to begin writing for over ten minutes."

In most religious Orders and Congregations, the use of the discipline is regulated by rule or by custom, and subjects ought to respond to such regulations with generosity. But it must be carefully understood that this violent penance, so far from dispensing from small mortifications of body and of spirit, ought, on the contrary, to make us more courageous in practising them. It is logically absurd to take on great, voluntary macerations, and then to dispense oneself from the smallest mortifications. Yet, this state of affairs is often found.

All the biographers of St. Thérèse of the Child Jesus have noted that she suffered greatly from cold, right up to her death. That is why the saint did not hesitate to make reserves to the observance she had accepted so heroically. " She considered," says her Autobiography, " that not to take account, in the observance of the Rule, of differences of latitude and diversities of temperaments, was to tempt God and to sin against prudence."

However, the opposite excess, of according too much to nature, must be avoided. To take an example: if a man has a bed in a room which is centrally heated, and takes care to supply himself with soft linen and a hot-water bottle, he can arrange for himself, in spite of some passing, self-inflicted disciplines, quite a soft and comfortable life. St. Vincent Ferrier writes: " While observing ordinary prudence, a servant of God ought to avoid an over-comfortable bed."

To one of the Sisters, who had placed her sandals on a heater, Soeur Thérèse said: " If I had done that, I would consider myself guilty of softness." Similarly, she would not allow a novice to fasten the sleeves of her habit with pins, against the cold. It is understood, of course, that charity ought to make us offer and even impose on the sick and the aged, all the comforts which their weakness demands. But here again, the extreme must be avoided. If certain people in a community have need of certain comforts, that need is not to extend to all comforts. To learn what is the golden mean, we must put ourselves to school to the saints.

St. Teresa of Avila teaches that it is an illusion " to flatter ourselves that we are spiritual, and at the same time to take good care that we lose no tittle of earthly repose for body and soul. Not thus do we arrive at liberty of spirit. I can never admit such a method of spiritual advancement. I cannot believe it is good. This I know from experience, and I would always have continued in that miserable way, had not the Lord, in His goodness, made known to me a much shorter way."

The saint speaks from experience:

" Of what value is the body, our mortal enemy, if its demands prove the ruination of the soul? Let the devil see the faintest fear in us, and immediately he will persuade us that this, that and the other will destroy our health . . . weak as I am, I see myself always enchained, incapable of the least good, until the moment when I resolve to take no further heed of body or of health. God revealed this trick of the devil to me. If he raised the question of health, I answered: I care not if I die. I see clearly, that, though I suffered great infirmities, it was the temptation of the Evil One and my own remissness that caused me to yield, in many instances. In fact, since I began to treat myself with less care and delicacy, my health is much better."

A common objection takes the form: the health of people to-day has been weakened, and we can no longer impose on ourselves the observances practised by the ancients. We do not deny that there is a certain amount of truth in this. Notice, however, that it is quite a long time since this idea was expressed—as far back as St. Teresa of Avila, who, in speaking of St. Peter of Alcantara, wrote: " The world is no longer capable of such high perfection; our health is more feeble . . ." A person who makes any pretence to leading a Christian life, especially if he is not married, is in no way exempt from practising the counsel given by St. Augustine in that celebrated Rule which has served as foundation for monastic constitutions: " Master the flesh by fasts and by abstinence in eating and drinking, when health permits. When, however, one cannot fast, let him take care not to take nourishment between meals, unless he is ill."

This important precept concerns also those persons living in the world who lead a devout life, especially if they belong to a religious group. If they cannot fast, which happens so frequently to-day, they can at least deprive themselves of those little indulgences, those extra-between-meals, which they so easily allow themselves, and thereby they can follow the counsel of St. Thérèse that we should ceaselessly mortify ourselves in the smallest things. Be convinced of this—that, in what concerned herself, the saint much preferred " imitation to admiration," to use her own words. We pray to Soeur Thérèse, we ask many temporal favours from her, we heap roses and flowers about her statue, we burn blessed candles in her honour, but we never think of honouring her by devoting ourselves to sacrifice in little things. For she who said, in an audacious but theologically sound sentence: " There are certain trifles which are more pleasing to Jesus than the conquering of the world or even martyrdom, for example: a smile, a sunny word, when one is inclined to scowl or to show annoyance," will come more quickly to the aid of those who imitate her habit of little sacrifices, than to those who honour her with flowers, with candles and even with intercessory prayer. Perfection lies both in the exterior cult and in the method of little sacrifices.

We live in an atmosphere in which a certain mystical spirituality is honoured, and it is therefore necessary to stress the urgent need for the primordial and fundamental practice of asceticism. A specious and misleading mysticism—or misty schism—should not lead us to forget, that there never was and never will be another highway to perfection than the highway of the cross.

There are souls who impose long prayers voluntarily and regularly on themselves, even to the daily recitation of the Office, but who will not renounce a petty indulgence, or those long chattings and absorbing friendships so incompatible with spiritual advancement. Reflecting on these souls, St. John of the Cross writes: " It is truly lamentable to see certain souls, possessed of virtue and of divine gifts, loading themselves with spiritual exercises, while at the same time, they are cowardly refusing to end some paltry satisfaction, attachment or affection, which prevents them from progress to perfection." (*La montée du Carmel Livre* 1er, *Chap. VIII.*) Such souls should consider well the principle of the same holy Doctor: " Consider well the deplorable ignorance of these people. They freely choose to perform ill-proportioned penances, but they deceive themselves if they neglect the mortification of the appetites in all things. If they applied to ordinary self-renunciation half the energy they bring to self-chosen penances, they would make more progress in a month than they " now do in many years."

We are convinced that one cannot be too deeply penetrated with this golden rule of the spiritual doctrine of St. John of the Cross and of Christian tradition, which in our day has been so gloriously lived by St. Thérèse of the Infant Jesus. We know from much experience that many souls, vowed by their state or by free choice to perfection, fail to devote themselves to renunciation and sacrifice, and therefore we believe with Maritain : " We are dying of insipidity and self-complacency . . . of a religion which we have whittled to the measure of our souls. . . . What we need from St. John of the Cross is his uncompromising doctrine, and his example of complete self-renunciation."

We have made an exception, above, in favour of the aged and infirm: but such should be careful not to relinquish an acquired habit of spiritual and even corporal mortification.

We have said, and it bears repetition, that the fervent Christian must practise abnegation of self, both in body and in will, right up to the moment of death. Soeur Thérèse has given us a glorious example of this in her own life. She drank, drop by drop, the most revolting medicines, she asked for no comforts except such as were really necessary. On the eve of her death, she sent her worn-out Sisters to bed, and did not seek any attentions which were not absolutely necessary. Without rising to such an heroic degree as St. Thérèse, there are yet many mortifications which the sick should practise.

It is to be expected that Religious and people noted for piety should have so familiarized themselves with ascetic exercises, that they know how to accept without apprehension, with ease even, if not indeed with joy, the discomforts of sickness. Of course, it is true that a sick man is often not master of his nerves, but, thanks to a habit acquired in the school of small, daily sacrifices, an ascetic ought to be able to curb the impatience of his senses and the revolts of his nature. The spirit of penance he has cultivated ought to cause him voluntarily to submit to the hardships sickness brings.

It is unnecessary to stress that people who are young and healthy ought to apply themselves energetically to the practice of asceticism, in order that they may correct their faults and make progress in mental prayer. They are advised, in the early stages, to give their full attention to mortification, in order that they may realize in themselves the image of Jesus crucified. " In the beginning," says St. Thérèse, " zeal for others is a hindrance, and the soul loses by such zeal. It should have a care for itself only, and it will be of supreme value to such a soul to live as though it lived alone on earth with God alone." (*Autobiographie*, Chap. XIII.) A great Benedictine monk, Mgr. Hidley, writes to the same effect: " The less a monk thinks of converting the world and the more he thinks of converting himself, the sooner the world will be converted."

This sentiment is not to be accepted without reserve, but it is important to appreciate the very great amount of truth it contains. Before a soul concerns itself with the conversion of the neighbour, it is absolutely necessary that it should have studied itself and corrected its faults. Very often it happens that pious persons and Religious, who set no limits to their sacrifices, ruin their health, shorten their lives by wearing themselves out in works of mercy, exercise no influence in converting souls, because they have neglected the preliminary step of correcting some fault—small perhaps, yet so obvious to all that it paralyses their apostolate. The more this fact of experience is meditated on, the more one realizes the necessity of paying great attention to this first stage, which St. Thérèse calls the knowledge of oneself—a necessity which is much more pressing for those who are destined for the apostolate, than for those whose life is to be spent in enclosure and contemplation.

We must ever bear in mind the precept of the Gospel: " He that is faithful in that which is least is faithful also in that which is greater; and he that is unfaithful in that which is least is unfaithful also in that which is greater." (Luke xx, 10.) Because a person has neglected to examine himself in detail and to correct himself, during all the years of a pious life, it happens that, side by side with great virtues, certain faults thrive without the soul being aware that they exist. " I am far from denying," says St. John of the Cross, " that much virtue can be found with much imperfection in the same soul . . . I say only that, without the correction of these imperfections, the true interior spirit is impossible, for then nature is at war with the spirit, and although the damage occasioned may not cause fear, nevertheless there is a regrettable dissipation as a result." (*Montée du Carmel*, 2ᵉ, *Chap XXI.*)

It is not our intention, for it would detain us too long, to analyse the faults which, unless they are carefully guarded against, will impede our advancement in perfection and hinder our apostolate. We shall content ourselves with enumerating the principal points on which we should constantly examine ourselves.

We insist immediately on the necessity of silence. A subject of Soeur Thérèse has deposed in the Process of her Canonization: "Her great means was silence. She learned it from the Blessed Virgin. Like Mary, she loved to keep all things in her heart, both her joys and her sorrows. That silence *was her power and the centre of her perfection* . . ." Spiritual writers are unanimous on the importance of silence. He who preserves silence, says the Scriptures, preserves his own soul, and a soul without silence is as a town whose gates stand open to the enemy. The Apostle St. James is even more explicit. " If any man offend not in word," he says, " the same is a perfect man." The General Chapters of the great monastic Orders make the law of silence one of their principal concerns.

This goes to prove two things: that Superiors and Religious grown old in experience have constantly and in every age underlined the danger of useless conversations; and that it is harder than is generally believed to be faithful to the rule of silence. When a Superior visits a monastery to tighten a relaxed discipline, he is regarded as having succeeded, if he re-establishes the strict observance of the rule of silence. Suffice to remember the text from St. James: " He that sins not in word the same is a perfect man." But it is true in general that the pious person and the Religious, who do not fail in the observance of silence, give proof of a rare strength of soul—the result of such a fidelity to graces received as will render them worthy to receive grace in yet greater abundance. One of the most frequent recommendations of Soeur Thérèse to her novices was: " Those who observe silence are the happiest, because silence brings so much good to the soul, in that it prevents many faults against charity and so much trouble of every kind. I speak very specially about silence, because it is the point in which so many fail."

Kindred to silence is the curbing of curiosity. All the saints made a pact with their eyes, and they observed it with a rigour that seems exaggerated to us. St. Bernard, after many years of monastic life, did not know whether the apse of the chapel was lighted by one or several windows. A rigid observer of religious poverty, he once shocked his disciples by the rich trappings of the horse on which he had ridden. . . . Absorbed in prayer, he had not even noticed the luxury that had caused a scandal. St. John of the Cross said to his travelling-companion: " We are not travelling to see, but not to see." St. Catherine, when in prayer, yielded to natural curiosity and looked to see which of the Sisters was passing by. Immediately, the grace of contemplation was taken from her. She accused herself in great sorrow to her confessor, and even re-proached him for excusing her so easily of what she con-sidered a grave fault. Indeed, no one could count all the graces of fervour of which one is deprived, and all the temptations and even grave faults which are occasioned, by giving curiosity a loose rein. Curiosity and talkative-ness cannot be reconciled with regularity of life. We must now pass on to other causes of irregularity, for example, a passion for reading, a desire to finish a work commenced, etc. Reflection on these things shows the immense advan-tage of rigorous observance, for the acquiring of this habit means the death of many unsuspected imperfections. Soeur Thérèse, whose teaching we follow so closely, made a resolution, which cost her something to keep, that she would cease reading immediately when the time assigned to that exercise had finished. In Carmel, her elder sister used to admire that exactness, and she preserved a note

of her sister's which remained unfinished because the bell
had sounded when but a word or two could have finished
it. One day, a Sister continued to note a pious reflection
after the signal had been given. Soeur Thérèse said to
her: " It would be more valuable to your soul to have
left that, in order to observe perfect regularity." The
young saint, by this simple reflection, showed that she
had experienced and weighed the full importance of
minute fidelity to the rule.

It is obvious that this fidelity preserves us from many
grave imperfections. . . . Thus, it is a known fact that
particular attachments, so frequent and ordinarily so
regrettable, will not be formed or at least will not be
harmful, if they do not occasion prolonged chattings,
meetings at forbidden times and other failings in discipline.
All spiritual writers without exception have shown a
severity which sometimes astonishes the ordinary man by
its vehemence, in condemning these particular attachments.

" What will become of me," says Soeur Thérèse, " if,
as worldly people think, I have been the plaything of the
community. Perhaps, instead of seeing Our Saviour in
my Superiors, I would have seen only the creature, and
my heart, so well guarded in the world, would in the
cloister have taken on some human attachments. Happily
I was preserved from that real evil."

We have quoted the above from the *Histoire d'une âme*
to show that one must be merciless on oneself with regard
to human affections. Both St. Teresa of Avila and St.
Vincent de Paul spoke even against family ties, so natural
but so dangerous for religious souls who wish to belong
entirely to Jesus Christ. " Detach yourself from all
creatures," says St. John of the Cross, " and, in an especial
degree even, from your relations, lest flesh and blood gain

strength through the natural love which exists always between the members of the same family, and which it behoves one constantly to mortify in order to arrive at spiritual perfection." An objection can be raised that Soeur Thérèse did not feel herself drawn to imitate those saints who did not love their families. . . . Doubtless, but there is question here of a too natural affection. It suffices to recall the sacrifices she herself made. We read in the process of Canonization: " When her sister, Céline, entered into the cloister, she embraced her and went away immediately, though the Mother had given her permission to accompany her sister to her cell. . . . When her cousin, Soeur Marie de l'Eucharistie, was clothed with the habit, she deprived herself of the pleasure of accompanying her to the door of the cloister to greet her aunt, who had so often taken the place of a mother for her." Soeur Thérèse admitted that she deprived herself of this consolation because she had inordinately desired it.

Here, we recall those apparently unfeeling words of the Gospel: " He who hates not his father and mother and wife and children and brethren and sisters, yea and his own soul also, cannot be my disciple." (Luke xiv, 26.) Add to this, the equally arresting text of St. Matthew: " If thy hand or thy foot scandalize thee, cut it off and cast it from thee; if thy eye scandalize thee pluck it out and fling it from thee." In the course of our life circumstances will arise in which this doctrine must be applied to the letter by mercilessly imposing on ourselves the most severe privation; but it is especially in the first years of the spiritual life that this night of the senses, to use the expression of St. John of the Cross, must be heroically endured. In some cases, it is good for people of certain generous temperaments, to make a radical sacrifice of all things, to leave their relations without hope of seeing them again, to sacrifice the least natural attachment, to separate themselves from everything, even to the burning of those souvenirs to which people cling so tenaciously—in a word, to carry out such a complete destruction, that they can build on rock a supernatural house of sublime perfection.

Mortification of appetites and desires is of such primary importance that the question should be treated of in great detail. But it can be said that the difficulty is, in general, virtually resolved by the faithful practice of religious obedience. This virtue involves so much abnegation, that the only Vow taken in some Orders is one of obedience unto death. " Obedience," says Soeur Thérèse, " is the compass which cannot lead astray." Thus, obedience to a superior, to a confessor, to a director of conscience is one of the points on which souls who desire to rise to union with God ought to examine themselves most faithfully.

The sense passions weaken with age, or even disappear as a result of many curbings. Many virtuous Religious are known to have declared sincerely and simply to their confessors, that they found no combat in themselves against sensuality, sloth, jealousy, and so forth. . . . But self-love accompanies us like a shadow in our rise towards the Eternal Light. With pardonable exaggeration, St. Francis de Sales writes that self-love dies a quarter of an hour after ourselves. The struggle then is one unto death, and the sure way to victory lies in fidelity to the vow and the counsels of obedience. The Superioress of the Institute of the Sacred Heart who succeeded Mme. Barat and was the inheritor of her spiritual traditions, wrote: " The holy Religious will be she, who, aided by faith, by reason, by good sense, walks in the way of constant self-reformation.

In this way she will reach the complete emptying of self. It is this total abnegation of self which forms souls in total abandonment to the Divine Will." St. Ignatius gave this famous command to his disciples: *Perinde ac cadaver*— Obey like a corpse. Long before him, St. Francis of Assisi had used this simile of a corpse, in answer to one of his Religious who came to him for advice. One can criticize, of course, even from the point of view of Mystical Theology, the perfect aptness of this comparison, but it remains true in practice—and the lives of all the saints bear this out—that Christian souls who have attained to great heights of sanctity and have left mighty soul-sanctifying works as a testimony to them, have done so only by pushing to the verge of folly the virtue of Obedience, and by practising asceticism in great sacrifices as well as in the small sacrifices of every day.

CHAPTER TWO

OF HUMILITY AND THE GRACES IT WINS

HUMILITY, as St. Thomas has analysed it in the *Summa*, is a well defined and very special virtue. It is subordinate to modesty, which is in turn a part of the virtue of temperance. That is why the Angelic Doctor asks himself whether humility is the most important of the virtues, and answers that, in effect, it is, but that its order is after the theological virtues, the intellectual virtues, and the virtue of justice.

But it is important to distinguish between the virtue of humility, of which St. Thomas speaks, and the state of humility, with its much greater comprehension, of which the majority of the mystics speak. It must be carefully borne in mind, as we have indicated briefly in the last chapter, that the virtues, distinct and separate in theory, are in practice inseparable and even comprehend each other. The state of humility in a Christian ascetic or mystic presupposes always belief in God, confidence in His goodness, and virtually contains a prayer, tacit or expressed, imploring from God's mercy the pardon of past and present faults and His merciful assistance. This state of humility is commanded by charity, inasmuch as one wishes to practise the virtue for the love of God. The Christian soul which humiliates itself and strives for perfection, does so indeed because God has commanded it. The state of such a soul, then, is completely different from that of the philosopher or sage who would pretend to become perfect by an exclusive love of perfection or by obeying some categorical imperative.

What we have just said about Christian humility, such as the mystics practised it, is sufficient to show how, thus understood, it is complex and difficult to define. St. Benedict, in a celebrated chapter of his Rule, enumerates twelve stages of humility, but these stages, when examined, are found to comprise the whole of monastic life. St. Anselm distinguishes seven degrees, but with the same result. Thus, then, all authors are unanimous in proclaiming its capital importance. St. Thérèse writes: " The whole house of prayer ought to be founded on humility, and the more a soul abases itself in prayer, so much the more does God exalt it. I cannot remember having received a single grace of the great graces I spoke of, except at moments when I stood overwhelmed by the sight of my misery."

This quotation should make us understand very well how it can be said that humility is the first of the virtues: it is the pre-condition for the gaining of all supernatural graces. " God resists the proud, and gives his grace to the humble." The soul must humiliate itself that it may receive the divine gifts: strength, wisdom, faith, charity and mystical favours.

However, in practice, we must not separate the foundations and the superstructure of our spiritual house, because in the spiritual order all the virtues, says St. Thomas, are connected and mutually condition each other. " I wish to acquire the love of God through humility," said a pious soul to St. Francis de Sales—" And for my part," answered the saint, " I shall force myself to acquire humility through love."

That is why the greatest mystics—the author of the *Imitation*, St. Teresa, St. John of the Cross, Soeur Thérèse of the Child Jesus—in their teaching, which is really a transcript of their own personal experience, have envisaged the state of humility as a concrete and undivided reality, as something they have lived. They make no attempt to define or to systematize, but speak of humility as a very simple state, but one which theological analysis reveals as deeply rich.

In spite of this fundamental remark, it is true to say that humility is, in a general way, the first condition of holiness.

This truth ought to convince us that the strength necessary to progress in the spiritual life should not come from our own resources, but as a result of constant and humble prayer to God. The publican in the Parable who made his prayer: " Have pity on me, O God, for I am a sinful man," is the most arresting symbol we could find. For Christ teaches us that the publican was pardoned, while the pharisee, who relied on his fasts, his alms, his exterior religious observances, remained barren of grace, with the divine judgment pronounced over both: " He that exalteth himself shall be humbled and he that humbleth himself shall be exalted." This can be translated in terms fitting our context: " He that relies on his own resources shall be humiliated, but every man who humbles himself, by placing his confidence in divine help, shall be exalted."

In the preceding chapter, we have dealt with the necessity of correcting oneself, of mortifying all one's desires even the least details. But this, you may say, is an exercise of asceticism at once physical and moral which demands constant and even heroic energy. We do not question the truth of this observation, and our remarks would be addressed to a very small group of people indeed, if they envisaged only those who are naturally endowed with exceptional strength of character. But if, in practising humility as we understand it here—a practice which relies essentially on prayer and confidence in God—one acquires by divine grace supernatural aid, then any mortification is possible to the fervent soul: " I can do all things," says St. Paul, " in him who strengthens me." The Apostle speaks from experience. In a celebrated passage of the Second to the Corinthians, he confides to us that he has suffered humiliating temptations, which he calls buffeting given by the angel of Satan. He has thrice begged of God to be delivered and God has answered him: " My grace is sufficient for thee, for power is made perfect by infirmities. Gladly therefore will I glory in my infirmities that the power of Christ may dwell in me. . . . When, therefore, I am weak, then am I strong."

All the saints have realized this truth, but especially St. Thérèse of the Child Jesus whose life and doctrine rest on humility steeped in confidence. In a letter to her sister, Pauline, she writes: " Yes, I desire those wounds of the heart, those thorns which cause so much suffering. . . . I prefer sacrifice to all ecstasy." But where did she find the strength to bear valiantly those heart-wounds? In the humility of confidence which made her add: " It is my weakness which is all my power."

The references of Soeur Thérèse to this truth are found frequently in her autobiography, in her memoirs, in her letters, in the process of her canonization. " She counted solely," attests the T. R. Mère Agnes de Jésus, " on the help of the good God for everything. . . . She said that there was no other support except Jesus." Her sister, Céline, who, as a novice, had been under the direction of

Soeur Thérèse, said: " In the individual instructions which she gave to each of the novices, she returned constantly to this truth. You ought to rejoice in your failings, she said to me one day, for they are matter for self-humiliation. . . . When God sees us convinced of our own nothingness, He stretches out His hand to us." The contrary practice of relying on one's own strength, and on acquired virtues, she likens to leaning on a red iron.

We have already recalled the example of the publican. The denial of St. Peter is equally celebrated and even more significant. St. Thérèse meditated frequently on it. " I understand very well," she writes, " how inevitable was the saint's fall. He counted too much on the warmth of his feelings instead of *relying only* on the divine strength. I am quite sure, that had he said to Christ: ' Master, give me the courage to follow you even unto death,' that courage would not have been refused him." She poses the question—Why did not Our Saviour say to St. Peter: " Ask of Me the strength to accomplish what you desire," and she answers that Jesus allowed that fall, in order that St. Peter should be an example to all Christians of the need of leaning on God alone.

Soeur Thérèse, in her last sickness, said: " Ma Mère, if I was unfaithful, if I was guilty of even the smallest infidelity, I feel that overwhelming troubles would come to me and that I would no longer be able to accept death." When she saw the astonishment this caused, she went on to explain: " I speak of the infidelity of pride. Were I to say, for example : I have acquired and can practise such-and-such a virtue—immediately, I feel, I would be assailed by the most pressing temptations, and I should certainly fall. To avoid this disaster, I have but to say humbly in the depths of my heart: Oh my God, I beg

of you not to allow me to be unfaithful." The high
esteem with which she regarded humility caused her to
look on it as the road of love. "The only means," she
says, "of making rapid progress in the way of love is to
remain always very little; it is thus I have acted, and
now I can sing with our father, St. John of the Cross:

> 'In humbling myself so low, so low,
>   I raise so high, so high my soul
>   That thus I may attain my goal.'"

Perhaps it may be objected that this cult of humility is
all very well for contemplatives, whose life is spent in the
cultivation of the passive virtues, and who, not being
destined for the active apostolate or for works of charity,
such as the direction of a school or a hospital, have never
to take personal initiatives.

In reading the lives of the great saints, it is plainly to
be seen that the more they gave themselves to works of
charity, so much more did they experience the need of
humility. It suffices to read the life of St. Vincent de
Paul to be convinced of this truth. Here is a saint who
was a mighty initiator, who laid the foundations of many
charitable institutions, and yet he carried humility to the
very edge of extreme. "No one," writes Pierre Coste in
Monsieur Vincent, "practised humility more than he did."
He recommended it to his disciples in a form we seldom
meet with in spiritual authors. He commanded them to
be humble, not only in what concerned themselves
personally, but also in everything that touched on their
own Congregation. His Company of Missioners was to
look on itself as "a small, a very small, even a paltry
company, the least and the last of all." One of his first
lazaristes, Guillaume Delville, published a work on the
history, the spirit and the organization of his Institute,
without the Saint's permission. St. Vincent was not at

all pleased. " I can scarcely express to you," he writes to the author, " the depth of the sorrow you have caused me. . . . To publish what we are and what we do is something absolutely opposed to humility." St. Francis de Sales, writing to the Religious charged with the Hôtel-Dieu de Paris, said: " The affection you bear to your community leads you to suppose that you have no need of reform. But take care. . . . True love of our houses should make us jealous for their real perfection, not merely for their reputation." One should be deeply penetrated with this teaching. Ordinarily, one makes it a point of honour to praise one's religious family, and, after all, this is quite legitimate if it is done with modesty; but it must yet be carefully noticed that a dangerous self-satisfaction often insinuates itself into such praise.

In a general way, all the founders of Orders have ceaselessly fought pride in all its forms, even in its most subtle. If anyone could be accused of lack of initiative, it certainly is not Madeleine-Sophie Barat who founded so many houses of education. She ceaselessly recommended the cult of humility to her daughters. " She hated pride," writes her biographer, Bougaud. " Ah! the self! Could I but catch it, I would strangle it, for there can be no truce in this war: one must conquer or die." She says: " In his old age, St. John would repeat constantly to his disciples: Charity, charity—love ye one another. I too shall spend my lest earthly years in saying to my daughters: Humility, humility—always humility."

This doctrine, which fervent Christians have learned from the Gospel, is not in accord with the theories of pagan and humanist philosophers on the cult of the human personality. Nothing could be more opposed to the stoic thesis which bases itself on the power of the will, than our doctrine. Descartes, from the first pages of his philosophy, teaches us to seek in ourselves the first principle of our conduct. The moderns have followed him in this. Emerson, one of the celebrated exponents of American thought, writes: " The man who stands by himself, the universe stands by him also." It is not surprising that some spirits, even among the most vigilant, affected by this naturalistic teaching, should find the doctrine of Christian humility an incomprehensible mystery. " At least in our Protesant countries," writes William James, " the individual is looked on as the ruler of his own conduct. . . . We have some difficulty in conceiving beings, who are reasonable and yet who regard it as a good thing to humble themselves; I admit that this is a mystery to me." Nietzsche, inspired by his hatred of Christianity, cursed humility on many occasions: " Above all, virtuous souls, you shall not walk on us. You would have us take humility to our hearts, but it is your own personal interests and a pitiable craftiness which commends your virtue to you. If you had more power and more courage in your souls, you would not abase yourselves to virtuous nothings." In perusing the works of Nietzsche, the theologian takes into account that German philosophy has never understood Christian humility. What must be borne in mind and never forgotten is that true humility, in abasing us, raises us up. This can easily be overlooked, because the majority of spiritual writers seem to emphasize only the crushing of the will.

St. John of the Cross writes: " If one wishes that God should bring about the union of soul with the divine, there is but one way of doing so: the way of annihilating one's powers according to their operation, the making of a void in the soul to give place to supernatural infusion and supernatural light." Indeed, Christian humility, in practice, is nothing else but the recognition before all of our nothingness, in order that we may find our strength in the divine. If sometimes the saint seems to act by his own power, it is still to do an act of good will before God, in such manner that his humble and constant attempt remains always itself a prayer in action. Soeur Thérèse, as always, explains this manner of conduct by an example which is very simple, but is the result of much experience. " Lift your little feet," she says, " to climb the ladder of holiness, and do not imagine that you can climb even the first step! No; but the good God asks nothing of you but goodwill."

The mystery of Christian humility, which exalts while abasing us, consists in this—that the soul, convinced of its own weakness, obtains by its good will the help of divine grace, when it undertakes any work. In emptying itself, it makes itself divine, by divine grace given to it. The supernatural power with which it is thus endowed does not suppress the will, but it gives so much smoothness to the ordinary action of the will that the will scarcely notices its own action.

It must be kept in mind that we speak here of the state of humility, which implies at least virtually, as we have said, the prayer of confidence; unwavering faith and divine love. This state of humility is extremely simple in practice, though in theory it can appear to be very complex, just as the purest light can be divided into all the colours of the rainbow in passing through the prism. Indeed, there is no other way than the way of a humility which is impregnated with confidence and the love of God, and which St. John of the Cross stresses in all his work, calling it the anagogic method. The explanation of this method has been given us by Père Elisée des Martyrs, a disciple of the saint.

Notice that the humbling of oneself by Christian humility and the exaltation through love are wholly one in practice, though these two movements seem self-contradictory. That is what those words of St. John of the Cross, in the verse we have quoted above, clearly imply. His symbol of the interior hiding-place into which the soul withdraws as a refuge from temptation, develops the idea more fully. " When danger threatens, the soul, seeing the demon approach, will thwart his purpose by retiring quickly into the deep secret place of its interior love, and will find security there. In vain does the demon let loose his terrors outside, for they seem but echoes to the soul within, and are an occasion of great joy to it." (Can. Spir. 11. xvi.) This hiding-place of love is also that of humility. In a temptation which seemed insurmountable to her, a novice said to Soeur Thérèse: " That time, I just couldn't risk coming out into the open." The saint replied: " Why do you wish to come into the open? Simply stay inside."

With St. John of the Cross for guide and inspiration, we will outline the anagogic method, which implies both humility and love. There are two methods of conquering vice and acquiring virtue. First, there is the ordinary method, which consists in combating a vice, sin, or temptation, by the particular virtue opposed to it. St. John makes use of the example: if I find in my soul a movement of impatience or of revenge, I consider the merits which are acquired by sweetness, and I meditate on the magnificent serenity and silence of Our Saviour before the Sanhedrin and before Pilate. This manner of acquiring virtues and of resisting temptation is good, says the saint, but it is slow and laborious, and presupposes that one has at least the time to reflect under temptation. The other method, which consists simply in opposing to the first movements of any passion a profound act of humility, which is at the same time an act of supplication, of faith and of love, is prompt, immediate, and supremely efficacious. St. John of the Cross writes: " Immediately the first movement of the first attack of a vice is felt, an act of the contrary virtue need not be elicited, as in the first method, but the soul should have recourse immediately to an act or movement of anagogical love which opposes itself to the movement of temptation." This act of love is also an act of humility. It is to be noted that this loving and confiding humility can defeat those temptations of the purgative way which are ordinarily met with by beginners in the spiritual life: lust, anger, revenge, etc. The soul, having taken refuge at the feet of Our Saviour in the crypt of prayerful humility, is in security from the enemy's attacks.

Sometimes the beginner is unable to elicit spontaneously such acts of humility and love, until he has first exercised himself by pious reading and meditation, to acquire these virtues; it can happen, even with souls advanced in holiness, that, by the divine permission, a temptation is so strong that it persists in spite of repeated acts of humility and adoration, and then recourse must be had to the contrary virtue or to meditation and suitable acts of penance. It is therefore advisable, according to the circumstances, to employ now one method, now the other, now both simultaneously. The more a soul advances in perfection, in the practice of humility, of faith, of charity, the more the mystical method of prayerful or adoring humility reveals its power. " The souls," says St. John of the Cross, " should have faith in the excellence and the efficacy of this method, being well persuaded that it unites all the means necessary and essential for victory in these combats."

We have, then, been instructed in the means of checking all our passions and our least disordered appetites; we know, also how we should put forth the effort necessary for the practice of constant daily mortifications. By exercising ourselves in detachment from all things and in self-abnegation, we shall prepare ourselves unconsciously to meet with victory the greatest trials which life may hold for us. We are ignorant of the future, and we know not if, perhaps, unjust and terrible persecution awaits us round the next turning of our years, to put our virtue to the severest test.

Our Lord warned His Apostles against all kinds of trial: he foretold that the time would come when whosoever pursued them with hatred or put them to death, would believe that he did a service to God. " Take heed what I say unto you. The servant is not greater than his master. If they have persecuted me, they will also persecute you." He sent his disciples as lambs among wolves; he warned them that they would be called on to practise and teach his doctrine in the teeth of war and appalling seditions.

We must not regard these evangelical warnings as addressed only to the first Christians. There has never been a considerable span of time in which believing souls have not had to face persecution and heresy. We must, therefore, be always ready. Submission to the Church or Christian humility is the only guarantee of our final perseverance. If they are not founded on humility, even the most exalted virtues, even the loftiest knowledge can cause the most lamentable falls.

With superficial and easy optimism, we are sometimes tempted to take for granted that the whole course of our life will have an easy tenor of social, intellectual, moral and religious peace. We borrow too easily the celebrated

phrase: " All this will endure as long as we endure."
On the contrary, what is infinitely more probable is that
all this will not so endure. This generation, says Our
Saviour, will not pass away till all these things be fulfilled.
In every case, we must be always ready to meet the most
cruel and most dangerous social and doctrinal crises, and
we can be ready only by the habit of constant mortification
in little things, and by the daily practice of humility and
prayer. It is absolutely certain, for example, that a Soeur
Thérèse would have walked imperturbably, with the
courage of the first Christians, to martyrdom, and that
she had an intuition of the anti-Christian tendencies of
certain modern doctrines which have acquired such
impetus since her death. It is not by " the will to power,"
but by Christian humility impregnated by the other
virtues of which it is the condition that the first Christians
conquered their persecutors.

The heroism of the martyrs of Lyon—St. Pothin,
Maturus, Sanctus and especially St. Blandine—is an
inspiration to us. Blandine was a poor slave, feeble in
health, so that her mistress feared for her perseverance.
But, says the Letter of the first Christians of Lyon, " in
her case, Christ showed that what is vile, unlovely,
worthless in men's eyes, is held in great honour before
God, who looks to real and strong love, not vain appearance. By the gift of the Holy Spirit, she suffered intrepidly,
from morning till night, sufferings and torments, any one
of which should, in the ordinary course of nature, have
killed her; sustained by her humility, the deep assurance
that she had of being united to Christ gave her not only
the courage to support unspeakable torments with joy,
but also to inspire to perseverance Ponticus, a boy of
fifteen, who suffered with her. All these first martyrs, who
were the founders of Christianity in France, were inspired

by the purest Christian mysticism; they continued the Passion of Christ of Whom they were the immediate disciples. The Letter of Lyon, a document of undoubted authenticity, is most sublime. Renan, who cannot be suspected of any partiality to Catholicism, writes:

" This letter is one of the most extraordinary fragments in any literature. Never has the degree of enthusiasm and devotion to which human nature can rise, been so strikingly shown. It is the ideal of martyrdom, with no shadow of pride in the martyr."

Add to these reflections of Renan that, by their heroic courage, they gained a definitive victory over the instinctive cruelty of the Gauls, who left the amphitheatre, struck with admiration and speaking with wonder of Blandine, the poor slave: " Never have we seen a woman so suffer," they said.

In reading the Acts of the first fathers of our faith, we have reason to be proud of their greatness of soul. That is why, when Nietzsche wrote in his characteristically brutal way: " Above all, virtuous people, you will not walk on us; we wish you your humility to your heart's content, for it is your own personal interest. . . . One must be a thoroughly petty type, if one has only virtue to show. . . . The men who mattered were never such jack-asses of virtue," he showed that he had no exact knowledge of humility. Reading the religious history of France, we meet with supernatural heroism arising from the humble virtues of the first Christians. " In confessing the faith," writes Jullian (*De la Gaule*, 206) " Blandine showed greater courage than the Emperor Marcus Aurelius in combating the barbarians." Where are such fruits of courage to be found in souls inspired by Stoic, Nietzschean or other doctrine based on pride?

It must be clearly borne in mind, and cannot be too

often stressed, that Christian humility at one and the same time abases and exalts the soul. The *Magnificat*, which is the hymn of the first and most humble of virgins, is both a song of humility and a paean of triumph. St. John of the Cross loses no opportunity in his mystical writings of recalling that two essential movements constitute the true Christian spirit: one which abases the soul, and the other which raises it above nature. St. Thomas Aquinas writes: " That a person, through confidence in the Divine assistance, undertakes works which exceed his natural strength, does not argue a lack of humility, especially when it is remembered that the soul is raised above itself by divine grace, in proportion to the degree in which it humbles itself. That is why St. Augustine says: " He who prostrates himself before God is exalted by Him." (2^a 2^{ae}. Q. 161, 2 ad sec.)

Philosophers and servants, less prejudiced than Nietzsche, and who, while not having the faith, have caught as it were an echo of the truth in their reading of the great mystics, have recognized the eminent value of humility.

" The dark night," writes Bergson (*Le Deux Sources*, p. 249), " is perhaps the most significant thing in Christian mysticism. . . . By it, the Christian soul purges from its substance all that is not sufficiently pure. . . . Now, it is God Who acts through it, in it: the union is total and, therefore, definitive. Such a one registers a change which raises him to the number of the *adjuthores Dei*, weak and passive with reference to God, strong and active towards men. The soul feels no pride in this elevation. On the contrary, its humility is great. How could it not be humble when it has experienced, in those silent communings alone with the Alone, and with an emotion which filled it entirely, what could be called the Divine humility? "

It may be asked from what sources are we to draw this Christian humility which is a Divine power in us. We shall not list them here: they are treated at length in the works of ascetical writers.

We shall add, because it is so often overlooked, a profound and very fruitful source of self knowledge. There are certain faults which have been transmitted to us by heredity, or which we have contracted from the atmosphere in which we live. We are the more ignorant of them because the people about us are unconsciously tainted with them and often consider them good. To study them, is indeed, to use Tauler's expression, " to enter into one's own depths." A German, an Englishman, a Spaniard, and Italian ought to study his own racial faults. A Frenchman, who aims at perfection, will find it useful to read the French historians on his ancestors. " Not a city," Caesar tells us, " which was not divided into two factions, party spirit was the breath of canton, of village, even of home. With this go an intolerable boasting, a lack of coherence in aim, a lack of strength in enterprise, a lack of grit in reversals, an extreme volatility, a superstitious religiosity, and no idea of rule and of discipline." (B. VI, XV.) Exaggerated as these criticisms may be, they point to the faults which have been noted again and again, though in faded vigour, by political and military historians of France. Taine was severe on his compatriots, but he was not wholly unjust. He accused them of an incurable lightness inherent in their race, of a lack of perseverance in wearisome but necessary duties, of indulgence in harmonious and sonorous phrases.

However, personal or collective faults are not the principal reason why very pious and saintly souls humiliate themselves before God. Because they have an appreciation of His presence, of the Divine goodness and power, they acquire at once a profound knowledge of their own misery and nothingness, and this whether they have preserved their Baptismal innocence or won it back, since they realize that to God must go the credit for all the good that is in them. They regard themselves as very poor, or indeed useless and botching instruments in the hand of God. They know that they do not correspond with grace as they should, and they accuse themselves of many and grave sins of omission. Without reflection, they keep their souls constantly in a state of loving prostration before the Lord from Whom they look for help with the most firm confidence. In reading the biographies of the founders of the Religious Orders and of the great reformers, we are amazed at their profound humility.

And this humility, with all the sweet virtues which it supposes, has in no way impeded—we *cannot* stress this sufficiently—their boldness of initiative and the fruitfulness of the apostolate. The saint who is always cited as the type of humble meekness, St. Francis de Sales, took on alone to convert the obstinately heretical country, le Chablais. The beginning of his apostolate in that region was marked by a series of heroic acts, which his father, M. de Boisy, not unreasonably judged as savouring of presumption and rashness, from the view-point of human prudence. " Your zeal," he wrote to him, " can end in no good. Your perseverance is an unreasonable obstinacy. . . ." But neither the contradictions of his relations and friends, nor the stubbornness of the heretics, nor rain, nor snow, nor ice, nor terrible storms could daunt St. Francis de Sales.

We meet many examples of such heroism in the lives of the saints. Though often feeble in health, frequently tried by grave sickness, they have surmounted a thousand difficulties and conquered all obstacles, so that their lives, when studied closely, appear as continual miracles.

If we are profoundly humble, and if that humility is joined, as it ought to be, to faith and charity, we need have no doubt that we, in our measure, will attain to something of the achievements of the saints. " Verily," says Christ, " he that believeth in me, the works that I do he also shall do, and greater than these shall he do." (John XIV, 12.) When circumstances demand heroism, when persecution and schism raise their heads, then humble and sweet apostles of Christ will not be wanting, who, if they cannot conquer their persecutors and contradictors by force of reasoning, will convert them by the compelling eloquence of their mighty example, and, if necessary, even by the supernatural power of miracles.

CHAPTER THREE

PRAYER—VOCAL AND MENTAL

THERE can be no easing off of effort in the spiritual life of souls who tend to perfection. To acquire a knowledge of their faults and the strength to correct them, they ought, we have said, to keep themselves in a state of profound humility and confidence in God, but they ought also to use the different kinds of prayer, that they may obey the precept of Christ: " We ought always to pray and not to faint."

The most elementary method of prayer is the repetition of the same formula, as in the *Pater*, the *Ave*, the *Gloria Patri*, etc. For centuries now, the most popular of vocal prayers is the Rosary; but it must be remembered that the *Ave Maria* was not always used in the Church. The Psalms of David were traditionally used, as they are still used to-day by Religious, priests and certain pious people; but with the passage of time and the changes it brought, Latin ceased to be commonly understood, and thus it came about that many Christians were using a language of prayer which they did not understand. This was a great triumph for the unbelievers, who were not slow to scoff at such repetition as verbiage, and to mock at prayer as senseless babbling. We have even heard the recitation of the Rosary identified with the mechanical whirr of the spinning-wheel and the rat-tat of the machine-gun.

Clearly, it does not require much intelligence or imagination to ridicule this humble practice. With some surface culture and without taking the trouble of reflecting on the matter, one can see nothing in vocal prayer but an opiate which dulls, when it does not altogether suppress, our intellectual faculties. A famous saying of Pascal in this connection may even be quoted: "Naturally, this will stupefy you."

We have remarked how easy it would be to indulge in a thousand witticisms on this subject, but, if one takes the trouble to study the history of our religion, it will be found that many great souls—St. Augustine, St. Thomas Aquinas, St. Francis de Sales, Pascal, Bossuet, St. Teresa of Avila, etc.—were given to that kind of prayer. Now, it was by a free choice they did so: it certainly cannot be suspected that such intelligences, so mighty and so conscious of themselves, did not reflect on the benefits of this practice as much, and more, than the smatterers and even the cultivated spirits who belittle it.

It will suffice if we convince ourselves, once for all, that the religious or mystic soul compels itself to maintain, even by the use of physical means, that state of humility, of confidence, of faith, of love of God, of indulgence and charity to the neighbour, which we have studied in the preceding chapter, and which constitutes the true Christian spirit, so seemingly complex and yet so simple.

It has been said that we must not pretend to play the angel: the Catholic mystics, who were complete and balanced people, appreciated this more than anyone else. "We are not angels," says St. Teresa, "we have a body. It is foolish to wish to play the angel on earth; ordinarily we need a prop to thought; sometimes the soul will be so filled with God that it will have no need of created things in order to recollect itself, but this is the exception." (Vie, Ch. XXII.)

Prayerful humility which is so necessary to the Christian soul can, in many circumstances, be practised in its pure state, if one may so express it, but this state cannot endure always nor even for a long time with man, without the aid of physical practices. Hence arises, with the ascetics, the habit of having recourse, according to the temperament of each, to prostrations, to genuflexions, to inclinations repeated a hundred times, and also to those prayers a thousand times repeated, which keep alive the sentiment of self-abasement, of adoration and love of God. The critics, inspired by a shallow spirit or by learning which is wholly quantitative, can have no knowledge of this intimate religious life.

It has been said, in a passage which still passes muster though certain reserves must be made: " When a criticism or apologia of a religion is made, does one always take account of what is specifically religious in the religion? One defends or one attacks the recitals of which perhaps the religion has need in order to obtain a state of soul favourable to its propagation; but religion is essentially that state itself." (Bergson, *Les deux Sources*, p. 290.) In this sense, Our Saviour said: " My religion is spirit and life." If one wishes to understand Christianity, it is the spirit and the life of that religion that must be examined. What answer is to be given to a Religious who has recited his Office without understanding the Latin of the Psalms, who has spent a half-hour saying his Rosary without attending to the sense of the words, if he assures us that he feels better for it, more recollected, more humble, more resigned, nearer to God and more concerned for his neighbour?

It is a well-established fact, however, that the pious soul has often, by a divine gift or by some kind of intuition, a knowledge of obscure texts which it reads. Cassian, a monk of the fifth century, has both experienced and thoroughly analysed this psychological phenomenon. " The *Holy Books*," he says, " offer to the mystics thoughts and sentiments which correspond to their state; we then understand the Scriptures more clearly, we penetrate them more. The Holy Spirit, with a clarity which surpasses all human explanations, suggests in advance of the meaning, so to speak, the words and their content; the sentiments which animate the author of the psalm come into our hearts, so that we seem to become ourselves the author of the psalm, meeting his mind rather than following his thought, in such wise that we understand the sense of the verses before we understand their language."

This harmony between the state of soul of the inspired writer and that of the fervent Christian makes us understand how the latter, by seizing vaguely on a word, can understand the whole sense of a passage in a psalm. The Curé d'Ars never succeeded in learning much Latin, and nevertheless he delighted in the recitation of the Breviary. " What happiness," he cried, " to be able thus to relax a little. . . . When I think of those beautiful prayers, I am tempted to cry out: happy fault! since if David had not had those sins to deplore, we would not have had the prayers. . . . The Breviary is my constant companion; I shall go nowhere without it." It will perhaps be remarked that the Curé d'Ars and many saints gave meanings to the sacred texts which were not in their author's mind. That is true. But it cannot be held that that was always so. It has often happened that the mystic has understood better the primitive sense of the inspired book than the philologist, who strives to translate literally a text somewhat deformed by long usage. St. Teresa writes: " In the prayer of quiet, I experienced a strange thing. Though ordinarily I understand scarcely anything in the

Latin prayers and especially in the psalms, nevertheless I sometimes understand the Latin verse as if it were in Spanish; much more than that, I discover with joy its hidden sense." That this hidden sense was that intended by the author or not, is of no importance to the question of which we treat. When Pascal declared that he found in Psalm 118 ever new and admirable truths which thrilled him, it is very probable, if not indeed certain, that his genius coloured the psalmist's thought with its own conceptions, but this meant only that the recitation was even more profitable to him. Besides, mystical authors have foreseen these personal interpretations of their words, and they have deliberately left a wide liberty to pious souls. It is thus that St. John of the Cross, interpreting the strophes of his " Spiritual Canticle," writes: " When there is question of words of love, it is best to leave each reader to draw from them according to his dispositions. If the explanation is confined to one precise sense, it ceases to be of use to all. In my comment, I give precise explanations, but I do not intend these as the unique meaning that can attach to my words. Mystical wisdom, indeed, needs not to be distinctly understood in order to produce divine love and generous movements in the soul." (*Prologue.*)

In treating of vocal prayer, we have unconsciously passed on to mental prayer, but this is quite natural, since vocal prayer, to be of any value, must be united with mental prayer. " It is not essential to mental prayer that we should pray in silence," says St. Teresa. " If, when I pray aloud, all my soul is occupied with God; if I keep myself in his presence, more attentive to that Presence than to the words I say, then I unite mental and vocal prayer in the same prayer. Let no one pretend to speak to God, if in saying a *Pater*, his mind is occupied with the world."

The holy Curé d'Ars felt compelled, at least for many years, to recall a scene from Our Saviour's Passion before reciting an important part of the Breviary. He even asked one of the confidantes of his secret, Catherine Lassagne, to write in the margin of the hours of his Breviary the corresponding mysteries of the Passion: for example, the Agony in the Garden for Matins; Jesus scourged and crowned, for Prime; Jesus condemned, for Tierce, etc. St. Francis de Sales also adopted this method, and we know that it is essential to the proper recitation of the Rosary that we should meditate on the mystery assigned to each decade, as we say the ten *Aves*. The Rosary, however, is a devotion that has evolved; in the beginning, a much greater latitude was given to the faithful in the choice of mysteries, and they could use the entire time of reciting the Rosary in thinking of some one fact of the Life and Passion of Christ.

This method of prayer introduces us to meditation and even to prayer, properly so called, and therefore to the contemplative life. This is a point to which St. Teresa of Avila loved to return, and on which she has written with great mastery.

" I know many people," she writes, " whom God has lifted from the simple exercise of vocal prayer to sublime contemplation. One of them habitually used vocal prayer, and felt compelled, when she wished to pray otherwise, to have recourse to the recitation of some ' Our Fathers,' while she thought of some mysteries or of Christ's shedding His Blood. Yet in this way, she entered into an intimate union with the Divine Master. She came to me one day, greatly concerned because she was unable to make mental prayer or to apply herself to contemplation. I asked her what prayers she recited and I discovered that, in simply saying the ' Our Father,' she had been raised to such a height of contemplation that she had known union with the Divine. This being so, let not you who are enemies of the contemplatives, flatter yourselves that you are secure from becoming one, if you recite your vocal prayers with the attention and the purity of conscience which you ought."

This quotation should show us clearly that vocal prayer is in fact, and without certain souls knowing it, often intimately united not only to mental prayer, but to contemplation. Above all, if we consider with St. Teresa that a soul can enjoy the prayer of recollection, the prayer of quiet or of union during the space of a *Pater*, we see how difficult and even impossible it is to distinguish in fact between the ascetic life and the contemplative. It is, however, to the ascetic life that we must give our attention in these early chapters, and meditation, properly so called, is incontestably in the domain of the ascetic.

Meditation on the virtues, the mysteries, the principal events in the life of Our Lord, of His Apostles, and of His saints is certainly necessary for Christian souls who are anxious to make progress in the way of perfection. Not only must they be faithful to this practice in the beginning, but they should know how to return to it at any time to the end of their lives. St. John of the Cross, one of whose aims was to raise the pious soul as quickly as possible from meditation to prayer and contemplation, takes care, nevertheless, to stress that meditation is indispensable. " The practice," he writes, " ought to be continued as long as it is found useful, and that under pain of losing ground: great care must be taken not to leave it aside too soon." This statement is of a nature to discourage many souls who think that they cannot meditate and that they have never succeeded in making a regular meditation. It could be answered, of course, that they have not applied themselves with the earnestness they should to this exercise. However, since a regrettable misunderstanding can arise between these souls of good will and their director, it must first be made clear what one means by meditation. At the word *meditation*, devout people envisage a highly complex exercise of the mind, by which they are required to choose a subject, to divide that subject into many points on which they successively exercise their different faculties, the whole having been prepared for by a period of reading to which they devote themselves beforehand that they may gather fruit for reflection and make suitable resolutions.

It is true that meditation, since the sixteenth century, has been regarded as made up of these things. They who have the time to adopt them, and who can accustom themselves to them, will draw from them the greatest fruits; but before the sixteenth century and without such rigorous rules, fervent Christians gave themselves to meditation. It cannot be doubted that the Fathers of the Desert, that St. Dominic, St. Francis and their disciples constantly used this form of prayer; it evidently follows, therefore, that one can and indeed ought to understand the word meditation in a very wide sense that will make its practice accessible to a very great number of souls. Firstly, as we have already said, to recite the Psalms or certain prayer formulae while the mind is occupied with the consideration of some virtue or of some mystery of our religion, is, in the wide sense, to meditate. To read slowly the work of a spiritual writer or even the life of a saint, pausing now and then to allow one's mind to be impregnated with the virtues taught or the examples given, is also to meditate. St. Thomas Aquinas ordinarily used for spiritual reading the " Conferences of Cassian," from which he received, he tells us, rest of spirit and a renewal of fervour. Such reading was not, therefore, study for him, but true meditation. Similarly, St. Teresa based her spiritual life on her reading. Speaking of her first years in the religious life, she said: " I passed the greater part of my time in reading good books. They were the delight and the refreshment of my soul, God not having gifted me with the talent for reasoning. . . . Persons who are similarly deprived of this faculty ought to read a lot, for periods of reading, however short, are very useful and even necessary for them." The saint admits that for a long time, except after Holy Communion, she could not bring herself to begin prayer without a book. " Ordinarily," she says, " I did not experience dryness of soul, but I never escaped it when I was without a book." On the subject of reading, she says: " If souls incapable of connected or prolonged reasoning, meet a director who forbids them the use of a book, it will be impossible for them to obey him for any length . . . without useless exhaustion." It is essential, therefore, that a great latitude be given to souls, that very great attention be paid to their inborn aptitudes so that they may be directed in a way that suits them, and, finally, that a scrupulous respect be had for suggestions that have their origin in the gifts of the Holy Spirit.

The importance, the necessity even, of using spiritual books in general, not only those which treat of the virtues, but those also which unfold the life of Our Lord, of the Apostles, martyrs and saints, will be more deeply appreciated if we do not subscribe to the half-truth which regards meditation as an exercise to be practised at a fixed hour, during a certain period of time, after which a person is finished with it for the day. The morning meditation has been performed in strict accordance with the rules laid down, and so, without further thought, and with the feeling of a duty accomplished, one gives oneself to a multitude of occupations and good works. It is not thus that the role of meditation in the Christian life was formerly looked on. The Fathers of the Desert, the founders of Religious Orders knew that, during liturgical prayer, reading of Sacred Scripture, intellectual or manual labours, their meditation was not to cease. Similarly, under the guidance of the Holy Spirit and from a desire to deepen in themselves some virtue or the appreciation of some of the mysteries hidden in Christ, persons loving perfection will read and re-read a chapter from a spiritual writer or from the life of a saint, which answers to the most intimate needs of their souls. Such chapters, providentially met with, will nourish these souls, and they will be drawn to the chewing and digesting of them, in such wise that they will fill their days with fruitful reflections. In this context, St. Thérèse of the Child Jesus wrote: " Do not think that I float in consolations: oh, no, my consolation is that I have on earth no consolation. Sometimes, however, a sentiment like that which I drew this evening from the end of a period of very dry prayer, comes to console me: See the Master that I give to you. He will teach you what you ought to do. I wish to make you read in the book of life wherein is contained the *science of love.*" (Histoire, p. 208.) Soeur Thérèse, at this stage in her life, was fully occupied in perfecting herself in the virtue of charity. That is why she had not yet tasted of spiritual books which dealt with other subjects, and she would find herself in dryness of spirit as long as the word of divine love was withheld, which would free the brimming waters of charity in her heart.

It may be objected that the complete text of St. Thérèse, which we have but partly cited, seems to deny that reading such as we recommend is useful. She says: " Without showing Himself, without making His voice heard, Jesus instructs me in the secret; it is not by means of books, for I do not understand what I read!" It seems very clear, then, that the saint does not attach the importance to reading which we do. We answer, that it is also clear that certain passages of the *Histoire* must not be taken literally, and especially without taking the trouble to reconcile them with other complementary passages of the same book. It is true that Soeur Thérèse has written that, in the last years of her life, all spiritual writers left her dry and arid, because she read them without being able to comprehend their meaning. But in the first period of her religious life, she read and re-read certain works of spirituality. She applied herself always to plumb the depths of Holy Scripture: " In my failure to make meditation, the Holy Scripture and the *Imitation* came to my aid; in them I found a hidden manna, solid and pure. But it was the Gospel, above all, which sustained me in my prayers; from it, I drew all that was necessary for my poor, little soul. I constantly discovered new light, and meanings mysterious and hidden."

This quotation is calculated to give us a very just idea of what meditation ought to be. A text from the Gospel, from Holy Scripture, from the *Imitation* or from some solid religious writer, to which we have recourse in dryness of soul, can inspire us, especially if, as we have said above, it corresponds to an intimate and actual need of our soul. We reflect on it in a special manner in our meditation, but it remains virtually with us throughout the day. Let a particular piece of advice or exhortation be given us, or a page be read, or a word spoken in conversation which chimes with our preoccupation with this text, and perhaps the meaning which we were unable to penetrate at the hour of meditation becomes perfectly clear; it becomes like a bright light in our soul at a moment when we were least conscious of it, and causes us to see supernatural truths in a totally new way, through the divine aid given to us. This is undoubtedly the meaning Soeur Thérèse intended in the passage: " Jesus has no need of books or doctors to instruct souls. . . . Never have I heard Him speak, but I know that He is in me. At every moment He guides and inspires me; I see, just at the moment when I have most need of them, truths unknown till then. It is not principally at the hour of prayer that these truths dazzle me, but in the midst of daily occupations."

From certain diverse points of view and from different moments in meditation, it is equally true to say that a person should use certain books and should also know how to lay them aside; that meditation should be made at a fixed hour, and that it should be made throughout the entire day.

One cannot exaggerate the immense value of the life of meditation as thus understood. Natural knowledge, revealed doctrine, personal experiences, trials and especially the graces of the Holy Spirit will contribute to make us understand and live, in a more supernatural manner, the most important truths of the Christian religion. It is meditation, thus understood and practised, much more than the study of philosophical, psychological and theological works, which has given to the saints their profound knowledge of the virtues and failings of the human soul, of mysteries and in general of the most precious truths of Catholicism.

It has been stressed over and over again that without this vivifying meditation, Christian doctrine, even when presented with the highest art, does not produce the hoped-for fruits of conversion. This is what Soeur Thérèse recalls when she says: " Was it not from prayer that St. Paul,

St. Augustine, St. Thomas Aquinas, St. John of the Cross, St. Teresa and many other friends of God drew that admirable knowledge which has been the delight of the most learned? "

We have dealt with the different forms of prayer; vocal prayer, mental prayer, meditation. It may be urged that we have not dealt precisely with what is, properly speaking, prayer. However, we have not passed over it, since we recognize, with St. Teresa, that it is nearly always implied in the humblest vocal prayer and in meditation well made. The greatest among the saints have not sought out other prayers than the recitation of the Psalms, of the Rosary and Meditation. Some of them, if we can judge from their biographies and from their own writings, did not experience long, passive and silent periods of prayer, so ordinary with the great contemplatives. St. Margaret Mary remained a whole night on her knees in adoration before the Blessed Sacrament, without speaking or moving. There is nothing of this with St. Vincent de Paul. In the three-volumed " Life " by Père Coste, there is evidence only of Vincent's concern to pray well, to meditate well and to teach his sons and daughters to acquit themselves well in their vocal prayers and meditation. This meditation, however, with the saint and his disciples, was not merely discursive, but also effective. In other words, it implied prayer.

We seem to have recommended above all vocal prayer, reading, the life of meditation; but it must not be thought that we attach little importance to the half-hour of meditation prescribed in Congregations, Orders, and Religious Institutes. It can very easily be urged that, if souls who are entirely absorbed in a multitude of absorbing and exhausting works, do not make a regular meditation in the morning, it is highly improbable that they will meditate during the day. That is why it cannot be too strongly urged on these souls and on busy priests, that they should set aside a fixed time each day for discursive meditation. If they are faithful to this practice, they will receive special graces which will enlighten and fortify them in their application to good works, for their whole day will have become a prayer.

We have not dealt with the prayer of supplication. All the saints have had recourse to it, whether to obtain a spiritual favour or even a temporal one. We see Soeur Thérèse begging God for the conversion of a sinner, and asking too for an external sign to show that her prayer had been heard. Don Bosco and the Curé d'Ars prayed for the cure of the sick and infirm. The Christian religion counsels us to pray constantly, one for another. However, contemplative souls do not willingly undertake to present many petitions in their prayers, lest the concrete nature of these petitions should distract them from their union with God; they know, however, that the more intimate their personal union with God is, the greater is their value for the neighbour. St. Thérèse of the Child Jesus wrote: " Though I have only two brothers (missionaries) and my little sister-novices (four or five), were I to speak in detail of their individual needs, the days would be too short. Simple souls have no need of complicated methods. O Jesus, that word: *draw me*, suffices. . . . As a torrent draws with it all that it meets in its way, so the soul that plunges itself in the divine love draws with it all the souls united to it. In drawing me, Jesus, you draw the souls that I love."

Apart from intentions which are very specially recommended to it and for which it ought to pray, the advanced soul, wholly impregnated with the doctrine of the Communion of Saints, is attentive only to one principal thing:

its union, more and more intimately, with Our Saviour. They are deeply convinced that in accomplishing each day more perfectly the will of God; in loving, in suffering, in living constantly with Christ, they obtain greater temporal and spiritual favours for their neighbour than if they were to present a multitude of petitions. As St. Paul so energetically teaches, we form but one body, of which Christ is the Head. We are all linked one to another by unsuspected supernatural relations. " A soul which rises," Elizabeth Leseur loved to repeat, " lifts up the world." By vocal and mental prayer, therefore, provided it is an elevation of soul and union with God, we give forth a divine energy, the power of which is incalculable. To affect our fellow-men supernaturally by means of prayer and to obtain thus results which surpass all that can be imagined, it is not necessary to be a saint: it suffices that we know how to humiliate ourselves before God and to have an unshakable confidence in His mercy and His power. We recalled, earlier on, that remark of St. Thérèse on the difference it would have made had St. Peter prayed for grace to be faithful, rather than indulged in vainglorious boasting. We can reason in a similar manner about many parallel instances. Had the publican, hidden behind one of the pillars of the temple and not daring even to raise his eyes to heaven, prayed also for his family, his children, his friends, he would have been heard. When the good thief heard Jesus saying to him: " This day, thou shalt be with me in Paradise," had he too prayed for his own and asked the same mercy for them, Jesus would have granted his request. Thus, therefore, the power of a humble and believing prayer can never be calculated.

It may be objected that we beg the question, since the difficulty lies precisely in believing without doubting. We answer that faith itself is obtained by prayer. When the father of the epileptic child came to ask of Jesus the cure of his son, the Saviour replied: " If you have faith, all things are possible to him that believeth." Then the poor father, knowing the weakness of his wavering faith, cried out: " I believe, Lord, help thou my unbelief." Then Christ heard him and cured his son. Thus the whole discussion of prayer returns to the idea of that state of soul which is the foundation of our Christian piety—prayerful humility. To humiliate oneself in prayer, and to obtain by that humiliation a yet deeper humility, a greater faith, a more ardent and universal charity, a more intimate union with God—this is the principle of all our interior life, of our contemplation, of our fruitful action in the world.

Part Two

THE ACTIVE LIFE

CHAPTER FOUR

THE APOSTOLIC LIFE
*Its pre-eminence over the purely contemplative life,
when it is supernaturally enlivened by Prayer*

THE Christian life in perfection-seeking souls overflows
into action, and the need for an apostolate of action
is not slow to manifest itself, ordinarily, when the strength
of one's passions has been weakened. " Complete mysticism," says Bergson, " is indeed that of the true Christian
mystics. From their accumulated vitality, an energy is
given forth, a boldness, a power of extraordinary conception and realization. We have but to recall what a St.
Paul, a St. Thérèse, a St. Catherine of Siena, a St. Francis,
a St. Joan of Arc and many others have accomplished in
the domain of action." (*Les Deux Sources*, p. 243.)

This is indeed a striking historical fact: but it would be
a great mistake to suppose that souls, who have already
made some progress, should wait till they have attained
to sanctity or to an eminent degree of virtue before devoting themselves to good works or to the Apostolate. The
examples contained in the Gospel bear us out in this.
Doubtless the disciples chosen by Jesus were favoured with
exceptional graces, but, nevertheless, we see the Master
sending them to preach the good tidings in Galilee from
the very beginning of His ministry, when they were
evidently still very imperfect. The founders of the great

Religious Orders, St. Francis, St. Dominic, St. Ignatius, have done the same. After a sufficient period of initiation, they have immediately sent out their sons to conquer the world by preaching and by missions, and thus it was by the works of the apostolate that the majority of them attained to perfection and holiness.

Christians naturally inclined to a life of solitude have maintained, without giving sufficient thought to history and experience, that retirement and many years of monastic life are necessary in order to attain to perfection. This illusion was an obsessing scruple with the Curé of Ars. He did not wish to die a Curé, because, he said, he had never heard of a Curé being canonized. We are far from denying the mighty advantages of the life of monastic solitude, but it is too much to assert that one must enter a monastery, and especially a monastery of contemplatives, in order to attain to self-perfection.

A similar and more widely spread error is the belief that the most austere Orders are by definition the most perfect. " The superiority of a religious order," says St. Thomas, " does not depend on the strictness of the observances which it imposes, but on the suitability of these observances in view of the end intended." From this fundamental principle, he deduces that the first rank is held by those religious orders, which give themselves primarily to prayer, but are at the same time destined for the work of teaching and preaching. Why are such Orders superior to the purely contemplative? " Because," answers St. Thomas, " it is more perfect to give to others the fruits of contemplation than simply to contemplate, just as it is a better thing to let others have the benefit of our lamp than to keep it for ourselves alone."

St. John of the Cross, whose whole natural inclination was towards the mystical life of the anchorite, spoke as follows to his novices, as though constrained by the force of the truth. " Devotion to the neighbour is a fruit of the spiritual and contemplative life. The rule of Carmel implies," he went on, " care for the neighbour and concern for his salvation. The Rule has created a mixed life for us in a harmony of action and contemplation. What proves the excellence of this life is that it was the kind chosen by Our Lord. It follows, therefore, that the mixed life in religion is the most perfect."

The example of Our Lord which the holy Doctor brings forward is, when reflected on, a very suggestive one. Except for His meeting with St. John the Baptist, we know that the ministry of Christ was performed in an agreeable and wooded country, where not the Jews alone, but the Romans, the Greeks and strangers of every class congregated. Far from fleeing the world, it is clear that Christ sought out the most cosmopolitan towns in Palestine to announce His Gospel and to give clear and striking proofs of his Messianic power. It may be objected that this example of the Saviour is not for our imitation; but it is remarkable that at a time when an eremitic and ascetic sect like the Essenes flourished, Christ never counselled His Apostles and Disciples to retire into solitude; on the contrary, He urged them to action. On the day following Pentecost, the Apostles gave themselves to a most active apostolate and set off for the conquest of the world.

The vocation of souls who tend to the imitation of Christ and to perfection, should not be a general call to a solitary and purely contemplative life. Christ has given us an example in order that we should imitate Him; and St. John of the Cross makes a happy choice indeed when he cites the life of Christ as proof of the pre-eminence of the Apostolic life.

We have shown above why St. Thomas gives the pre-eminence to monastic Orders in which contemplation shows its fruits in teaching and preaching. Immediately after these came the Orders which are exclusively contemplative; and then the Congregations dedicated to external good works.

According to a principle put forward by Plato, and approved by elementary good sense, the most excellent things are also the most difficult. The religious life, in itself the most perfect, will therefore also be the most difficult. We are thus led to think of the mixed life in religion—by which we mean that which is in part composed of the apostolate of Christian doctrine—as the most difficult to practise well. This is a point about which many Christians are under an illusion.

We shall perhaps astonish some readers by saying that the devotion, so admired by the laity and even by unbelievers, which consists in giving oneself gratuitously to the care of the sick and young and aged, to teaching, is often much less meritorious supernaturally than is supposed. If a person is endowed in any degree with a generous temperament, he will be instinctively drawn to compassion for the unfortunate, and it is therefore relatively easy for him to be motivated by merely human pity and to cast himself into good works with heart and soul. This is doubtless admirable in the eyes of the world, but is far from corresponding to the ideal of Christian perfection.

It is certainly more difficult to leave the world in the manner of the fourth-century anchorites, and to live in solitude in order to devote oneself to penance and to contemplation; this act of renunciation demands a special vocation and a courageous obedience to the Divine call. We have often met the objection that, after all, the solitary and contemplative life is less difficult than the active. Of course, it is said, it needs a great act of will and of virtue to say good-bye for ever to one's family, and it also requires great perseverance to adapt oneself to a wholly new mode of life. But when one becomes used to it, this monastic life is very peaceful and allows the soul to taste the sweets of union with God. Those who speak thus, show that they have no experience, personal or acquired, of solitude. In the first years of his episcopate, Camus, Bishop of Belley, shared this mistake. Visiting a Carthusian monastery with St. Francis de Sales, he said: " How I would love the solitude of this good place." St. Francis answered: " Solitude is good when God calls us to it: otherwise, it is bad. You suppose that it offers less occasions of sin, but man finds himself wherever he goes, and misery dogs him like his own shadow." Solitude, even when one is divinely called to it, can cause an interior fermentation of the most base and most noble passions, and thus agitate the imagination and the heart of man. In this case, the solitary can defend himself only by turning aside to some external action; he stands alone, forced to combat his interior enemies—the most dangerous of all enemies, according to St. Gregory the Great. If one wishes to be convinced of this, it suffices to re-read what St. Jerome has confessed in a celebrated letter about the combats he experienced in the desert. He gives us to understand that solitude is an arena where temptations of all sorts take shape to haunt our days and our nights. That is why St. Benedict, in his Rule, would not allow his disciples to live an eremitical life until they had given proof, amid all the duties and work of a community, of having made great progress in all the virtues.

In spite of these considerations, we do not hesitate to assert that it is even more difficult to live conscientiously the life that is commonly called mixed, but which is, in reality, a contemplative life translating itself into action—the action of teaching and preaching Christian doctrine. The question, from whence does this difficulty spring, now arises. We can answer immediately in a general way, that the harmonious synthesis of complementary and apparently contrary elements is difficult to achieve, and, moreover, must remain relatively unstable, since an excess in any direction can destroy the balance. The active life and the contemplative life can both seem easy, but a union of the two with a predominance of contemplation is a complex and delicate affair. What a complicated organ is the human organism, says Pascal; and it is incontestable that the mixed life demands that one should use successively and together, all the relevant keys and stops of our many faculties.

This supposes that we have acquired a perfect self-mastery, in such fashion that we can submit our many passions and all our faculties to a discipline which is at once firm and supple. There must be no excess and no defect. Evidently, this mastery, of which the great apostles and the saints have given us such perfect examples, demands, with God's help, a preparation and also a constant self-vigilance.

It must be immediately noticed that, according to the aptitudes of each individual and the graces conferred on him, this synthesis runs the risk of losing its equilibrium, by reason of some inclination to give oneself with excess, and therefore exclusively, to one of the particular forms which compose the synthesis. We meet such tendencies, which become subtle temptations, even among the saints. St. Teresa of Avila was a many-sided and very rich character who attained to a very complete supernatural life, yet kept always a tendency, dangerous even, to an excessive warmth in her friendships. St. John of the Cross, who professed, as we have seen, an undoubted preference for the mystical and apostolic life, kept throughout his entire life a spontaneous inclination towards the eremitical life. The same is true of St. Francis of Assisi, who used to retire frequently with one companion into the mountain, and who would have given himself entirely to that solitary life, had not Br. Sylvester and St. Clare both counselled him to return to his preaching.

This attraction towards the contemplative life is much commoner than is supposed, among pious souls, but with the majority of them it is a form of deception. It gives the illusion of having a true vocation for contemplation, for prayer, for detachment from all things, for submission to an austere discipline, but such feeling is a mirage which never has power to inspire effective decisions entailing the realization of a project which is fitfully and lovingly fondled in the form of a wish-thought. With such beautiful wishing, one can live to the end of one's life, though protesting, in the whirl of the world and in lukewarmness of soul. Similarly, one meets with many Religious to-day who bitterly lament the multiplicity of their occupations, but who, on every possible occasion, cannot resist the temptation to quit their cells in order to give themselves, under the pretext of zeal, to superfluous journeys and to a life that is wholly exterior.

We touch here on a principal object which, with souls otherwise staunchly Christian, pious and religious, is opposed to that ideal life which we have attempted to describe summarily as action resulting from contemplation. The most difficult temptation to evade in all ages and especially in our own, is that which, under pretext of zeal and charity towards God and the neighbour, causes souls called to a superior and holy religious life, to fall into unrest and agitation. In many works of great talent and power—as in Dom Chautard's " The Soul of the Apostolate "—these souls have been warned over and over again against this modern danger; but, in spite of the success of these works, the danger is far from being removed. Many, indeed, have appreciated perfectly the value and the opportuneness of the motives alleged by these authors, but others have either not read them at all or quickly forgotten them.

When convictions are not matched with a life conformable to them, little by little they weaken and change, until, insensibly, we subordinate and make them comformable to the life we are leading, by a process of specious self-deception. It has been justly said: " We must live as we think, lest we think as we live." Psychologists of religion, of religious and of pious persons, have noted a tendency in recent years to canonize, so to speak, multiplied and fevered action, which degenerates into restlessness and is fatal to contemplation. Let us examine some of the most specious arguments for this kind of action.

In the first place comes the statement that it is a duty to sacrifice oneself entirely for the salvation of the neighbour, to spend oneself and give of one's full measure: but, if the phrase " give of one's full measure " is calmly considered, if it is analysed in the light of the elementary principles of Thomistic philosophy, it will be immediately evident that the phrase is equivocal. The question is whether " one's full measure " is to be understood in terms of quantity or of quality.

To give one's full measure from the point of view of quantity is evidently to multiply as much as possible the number of good works in one's ministry, and to pretend thereby to attain to perfection. But to conceive perfection thus, is to think of it as a *quantity*, and thus bring it from the spiritual plane to the material, for quantity pertains to matter. We do not hesitate here, in the manner of Socrates, to bring forward some homely examples. A woodcutter's worth will be estimated by the great number of trees he can fell in a day; a navvy, by the amount of earth he heaps; but surely one cannot assimilate the activities of pious souls or of persons consecrated in holy religion, to servile works like these, or measure their worth in the same quantitative way?

As the value of the occupation increases, the emphasis moves from quantity to quality. For example, it matters little if a talented painter produces a hundred second-rate canvases within a given time; what does matter is that he should create a masterpiece.

It can be easily maintained that this artist, in painting his hundred pictures, has not " given of his full measure," and, if he continues to work hastily, he will never give of it. His best will only come through greater concentration and more leisured execution. With even greater reason, in the spiritual order, it is not desirable that one should do a lot: the emphasis is on *well*-doing rather than doing, or, in other words, on acting supernaturally. A hundred mediocre sermons will not be as efficacious as ten which are prepared in prayer and study. Similarly, in a life consecrated to good works, an engrossed zeal which leaves an almost non-existent period for prayer, can inspire a devotion which will be the admiration of men, but because it is too human, it will not exercise that mysterious, effective influence which comes from the secret fire of divine love. It is usual to cite here the passage of St. John of the Cross: " Some spiritual people give the preference to activity and imagine that they can conquer the world by their preaching and their external works. Let them remember that they will render greater service to the Church if they use even half the time which they

thus fritter away, in prayer before God, because then they
will do more with less labour, and more by one prayer-
inspired work than by a thousand. To act otherwise, by
preferring only those active works which excite notice and
admiration, is to make noise, to do something which is
almost nothing, which is something absolutely nothing
and which may be even bad." This doctrine of St. John
of the Cross will be very clearly understood by those who
are familiar with the Pascalian theory and with that which
is traditional in Religious Orders. All the heaped-up
riches of the world could not of themselves give birth to
a single thought, for thought is of a superior order. All
the scientific inventions of the world together could not
cause a single act of Christian charity, for this is of
another world—the supernatural.

When it is said, and very rightly said, that it is the duty
of every man to give of his full measure, care must be taken
that not the quantity of good works only, but above all
the quality and the order to which they belong, are borne
in mind. Even from the purely human standpoint, he
who is satisfied always with numerous and mediocre works
when he has it in him to produce a few excellent ones, will
never give of his measure. With much greater reason, the
Christian or the apostle, whose whole life is absorbed in
works—social, humanitarian, literary—which are praiseworthy in themselves, but too human, will not give of the
full measure he could, were he to limit them, moderate
them, give more time to recollection and prayer, so that
his works would become endowed with a supernatural
and therefore infinite value.

Another objection, which reduces fundamentally to the
first, is that in giving ourselves to work and in renouncing
the silence of study and the apparent leisure of prayer, we
" seek out life." Here again, we must not be content with

vague and woolly words. We have a right to ask what the words " seek out life " really mean, because there are many kinds of life.

Man is endowed, says St. Thomas, with many different faculties, and according to these faculties we distinguish the physical life, the sensitive life, the intellectual life, the aesthetic life. He who loves movement in space and in time, seeks the physical life, and doubtless he can live intensely in this way, but by the use of faculties akin to those possessed by the animal. It is not those who get most rapidly and most frequently from one place to another who ordinarily have the greatest power for good over their fellow-men. Aristotle, and with him the Scholastics, said that the first Mover, giving life at every moment to all beings, remains Himself unchanged. *Primum movens immobile*. It is instructive to notice that in history the most powerful movers have often themselves remained almost unmoved. In time of war, the aides and the different liaison officers use much energy in covering great distances; but the supreme commander ordinarily remains quietly at his centre of command.

Thus it is that the most eminent life does not consist, as is often believed, in swift and frequent movement. St. Thomas teaches this clearly. Contemplation requires repose, but because it is an activity of the highest part of the soul, it is in man a superior life. This is true of purely natural contemplation, which is the consideration or the admiration in spirit of truth or of an assembly of truths; but, if this is true of contemplation which is confined to the limits of purely human faculties, how much more true is it of divine contemplation. It is a life which is not only intense, but transcendent. Plato, called the divine Plato by the Mediævals, has written in the *Banquet*, a page which is undoubtedly the most celebrated of ancient philosophy.

" O my dear Socrates, that which can give value to life is the vision of eternal beauty. How great is the destiny of a mortal to whom it will be given to contemplate the unshadowed good, in its purity and simplicity, not clothed in flesh and coloured with what is human . . . to see face to face, in its unique form, the divine beauty. Do you think that he who attaches himself to this contemplation will have anything of which to complain?" This superior form of life, which Plato only glimpsed and to which his disciples attained both seldom and fitfully, the great Christian mystics, aided by grace, have lived.

Without pretending to such perfection, the pious soul who meditates with love on the mysteries of Christ's life, and who is aided in his prayer by the Holy Spirit, also attains to a form of the wholly supernatural life. And since it is of the essence of good to diffuse itself—*bonum est sui diffusivam*—the most obscure soul, if it is filled with the fervour of divine love, exercises always a sanctifying apostolate. We conclude, then, that when a person says he seeks after life, it must be carefully questioned whether he means supernatural life or that life which is merely its shadow.

A third objection is drawn from the extraordinary lives of apostolic or active zeal led by saints like St. Dominic, St. Ignatius, St. Vincent de Paul. It will be urged in particular, that St. Eudes and St. Francis de Sales made a resolution never to refuse to preach, to hear Confession, to make a visit, when to do so was not absolutely impossible. St. Vincent Ferrer travelled Europe and preached for hours often and several times in the day. One cannot, therefore—it will be argued—preach or work too much.

A preliminary remark is called for. When extraordinary examples of penance or mortification given by some of the saints are quoted, the answer is promptly given that in this they are more to be admired than imitated, and we are careful not to deny this. The question is whether, in their extremely active apostolate, these saints are also more to be admired than imitated without reserve by us poor mortals. We have insisted that the life of a saint consists in a complex equilibrium or a harmony of virtues and of complementary gifts. Their example does not authorize us to practice immoderately the active life, if at the same time, we do not adopt their life of penance and prayer. It is true that St. Francis of Assisi, St. Dominic and St. Ignatius gave themselves to a many-sided apostolate, which was absorbing; but their practice of asceticism and their constant spirit of prayer were much more intense and admirable. It was thus that St. Francis de Sales never lost, from his maturity, the presence of God. He mortified himself constantly and in the least things, without losing an occasion for self-conquest. He ate but one meal a day, indifferent to what was served and drinking only water tinged with wine; he slept little; he took the discipline unto blood. He renounced his own judgment in all things, and, where no principle was involved, he acceded to the opinion of others. His prayer was continual, he recited his Office with the Canons in Chapter. " Often," he said, " I am so overwhelmed with affairs that I know not where to turn or with what to begin, but this does not trouble me in any way. I never experience distractions at the Office." It was the same when he celebrated the holy Sacrifice of the Mass. " Such was his attention," says St. Chantal, " that he was never distracted." He confessed always before Mass; he had vowed to say the Rosary every day, and he spent a whole hour in doing so, meditating on the mysteries. If the pressure of affairs left him no leisure during the day, he carried the beads on his arm to remind him to recite it before going to bed. We have listed these details—and the list could be of any length and from any saint—to show that, with the saints, prayer breathed on every part of their active life, making it supernaturally fruitful.

Finally, there is a point on which we would like to insist. We believe that quality and quantity, action and contemplation are not as opposed to each other as is generally supposed. Where human nature is in question, a working synthesis of quality and quantity is possible. He is greatly deceived who thinks that, by acting rarely and with very long preparation, he will produce excellent works from the point of view of religion. The proverb: *fabricando fit faber*, is relatively true, even in the Christian apostolate. One must preach much to learn to preach well, and similarly, if one is vowed by vocation to good works, such good works must be frequently performed to be well performed. Quantity, when it is not excessive, is therefore good and it improves the quality. In general, a fruitful apostolate of many and exacting good works, disposes us favourably to contemplation, provided always they do not absorb all our time and that they are not exhausting. Grave errors, even on the part of those who have studied spiritual and mystical writings, are frequent on this point. It is often after long experience only that one comes to realize the great usefulness of action. This was the experience of St. Teresa, who wrote: " I suffered from having little leisure to meditate, and I had great compassion for others whom I saw to be constantly occupied with the duties of obedience. I thought then, and I even said so at times, that I could not see how anyone could make much progress in perfection against such odds. But I have discovered my error; in particular, I have seen a person who spent fifteen years in constant occupations without ever having a single day to herself, so that it was

as much as she could do to steal some moments for prayer
and for the keeping of a pure conscience. God rewarded
her well for it; without being able to understand how it
happened, she found herself in the state of soul which
belongs to the most perfect. She is not the only such one
I have known . . ."

The saint, however, makes this express reservation:
" One should not give all one's time to good works except
through obedience, because otherwise it is preferable to
have one's moments of solitude."

This is what the majority of souls who allow themselves
to be drawn into a too active life, fail to do. They have
accustomed themselves to living in a kind of fever, which
they love and which they seek even while they deplore it.
They shun instinctively the state of recollection and peace,
which is a weariness to them.

In recent years, the urgent necessity to react against
this esteem and immoderate seeking after action is being
more and more realized. Many Religious and pious souls
have learned to be on their guard against this general
tendency towards exaggerated action. If this contagious
fever grows worse and reaches all classes of society, even
the clergy, then those who really wish to lead the contemplative life will have no alternative but to fly into
solitude, as the monks did in the fourth century. Perhaps
here is the explanation why souls to-day who are fired
with ideals, so often choose to enter the enclosed Orders.

This peril of fevered agitation which is nowadays so
contagious, and from which it is so difficult to escape in
certain atmospheres, does not weaken the general law we
have previously formulated. St. Thomas, following St.
Gregory the Great and the whole monastic tradition,
teaches that a well-ordered life of action disposes the soul
to contemplation, because it brings a harmony into our

passions and appeases the vehement desires which the obsessions of the imagination can cause.

This synthesis of quantity and quality, of contemplation and of action which constitutes the perfect Christian life, depends, as to its complexity and equilibrium, on our temperament, our character, the habits or virtues we have acquired; also and above all, on our vocation and the graces that are divinely assigned to us. But in every case, it is necessary that prayer should predominate in such a way that action is impregnated by contemplation—that it flows from contemplation as a stream from its source. Let us repeat, therefore, that the perfection of Christian life should not be sought in a life either exlusively active or exclusively contemplative, but in an harmonious synthesis of contemplation and action. This is what has been taught by the greatest Doctors of the Church, and practised in a wonderful manner by the apostles and the saints.

CHAPTER FIVE

THE STUDY OF CHRISTIAN DOCTRINE
*from the View-point of the Apostolate and of Personal
Sanctification*

THE doctrine which we have outlined concerning
prayer, meditation, action and prayer, supposes a
certain knowledge of spiritual ways and of religion. In
no case has a Christian attained to perfection and holiness
without having acquired sufficient knowledge, drawn
from tradition and from written and oral teaching.

From the beginning, we would make clear that it is
not our intention to deal in this chapter with the knowledge
the saints possessed—though many of them did possess
great literary and intellectual culture. When we are
dealing with the apostolate, it has been justly said that
we are not to confine ourselves to the knowledge necessary
to our own personal perfection, but must concern oursleves
with the needs of our neighbour. The apostolate exercised
through teaching, through preaching, through writing,
through works of charity, demands, according to diversity
of vocation, special and even professional knowledge.
Aside from these, the fervent Christian whose charity
leads him to desire the enlightenment of his neighbour,
should concern himself with the intellectual problems and
knowledge of his time, so as to have a sufficient knowledge
for his purposes.

An apostle like St. Francis de Sales, who was consecrated from the first years of his priesthood to the conversion of heretics, felt it his duty to have a thorough
knowledge of theology, and of those questions, in particular which were being disputed between Catholics and
Protestants. We read that he set himself to acquire
extensive and profound knowledge, that he studied the
Summa constantly, that he ceaselessly consulted Bellar-
mine's *Book of Controversies*. Hamon tells us that he read
the principal Latin and even Greek authors, and that,
by this classical education, he purified his taste, developed
his style and acquired an art of oratory which he found
valuable against the Calvinist preachers. The saintly
Curé d'Ars, however overwhelming his duties, made it an
invariable rule to re-read the lives of the Saints, and to
refresh his moral theology every year. . . . At this stage,
we can formulate one of the main ideas of this chapter,
viz., that the life of piety which we lead, however fervent
or even saintly it may appear to us, does not allow us to
neglect the duties of our state. True sanctity, indeed,
causes souls who have voluntarily assumed a charge or
employment, to appreciate how necessary it is for them to
acquire the knowledge that is required for the fulfilling
of that charge or employment.

It happens very frequently that devout persons who are
favoured with signal graces of prayer, are tempted to
believe that they need no longer read or study, but that
the intuitions of the Spirit are sufficient for them. This is
a temptation special to the saints, and, as we have shown
in the case of the Curé d'Ars, they know better than to
yield to it, for they appreciate that exceptional graces
do not dispense a person from working to retain knowledge
that has been acquired. The Doctors and the great
mystics teach that it is tempting God, if one acts as though

meditation and prayer can entirely take the place of study for us. It is true that, in exceptional cases, where the limitations of human nature have not been foreseen or remedied, the saints have been able to rely confidently on grace; but we, who follow the normal way of perfection, ought conscientiously to apply ourselves to gain the knowledge and the aptitudes required by the profession which we exercise.

Religious, priests and pious souls, to whom we address ourselves and who give themselves to the contemplative life, to the apostolate and to good works, have in most cases to fulfil obligations arising from their employment. It would take us too far to treat of the questions here; but it is sufficient to read the biographies of the saints to realize that their knowledge was much greater than is ordinarily supposed.

To be a saint, it is necessary to observe all that the moral virtues, and especially the virtue of justice, demand. We repeat that mystical favours do not dispense from the knowledge and the practice of the virtue of justice in all its forms—individual, domestic, social. Justice thus conceived, is so close to charity that it is hard to draw a precise line of demarcation between the two virtues. It can even be said that we cannot observe justice perfectly without practising charity; but it is even more true to say that it is vain to pretend to practise the counsels of Christian charity without having first observed the precepts of justice.

The duty of knowing well the precepts of the moral virtues is, therefore, a primary duty of the soul that seeks perfection. It is interesting here to recall some obligations, elementary ones indeed, on which devout souls do not examine their consciences with sufficient care. A lie should not be excused under pretext of safeguarding a great good, as, for example, the high reputation of a community or hospital. It is a rule, magisterially formulated by St. Paul, that we should not do evil that good may come of it. *Non faciamus mala ut veniant bona.* (Rom. III, 8.)

There is nothing original in saying that the religious life can lead souls into grave illusions, and it is for this reason precisely that sincere souls, fearful of pitfalls, put themselves under a spiritual director. The important passage of St. Teresa is well known, in which she recommends that confessors deeply versed in theology should be chosen, even if they are themselves not outstanding examples of spirituality. . . . Certain souls who are making progress in spiritual ways are tempted by the illusion that they can now ignore or neglect the least precepts of the moral law. It is unbelievable how easy it is to maim one's conscience, when one has no solid theological knowledge.

The immediate and most pressing knowledge, therefore, of a soul called to high perfection should concern the duties imposed by the ordinary moral law: for, so far from being dispensed by exceptional graces from the exact observance of its laws, the true mystic submits scrupulously to its minutest requirements. This constant conformity of our conduct to the precepts of the Decalogue and of honesty, is the necessary foundation of the science of the saints.

A Religious or a pious soul ought to know the Catechism as completely as possible. This knowledge supposes, not only the answers to essential questions, but also the ability to expound these questions. It will be thought that we are labouring an obvious truism here, but is it rash to opine that many pious souls know the elements of their religion but very imperfectly indeed? La Bruyère, the famous French character-writer, pokes gently at the preacher " who supposes that the great and beautiful world has reached a state of such refinement that it would be boorish to aim catechism answers at its head." Many pious souls would be very embarrassed if they had to explain, even summarily, the principal dogmas and commandments of Christian doctrine. It is true that even a very simple explanation of the Catholic religion borders on theological study, and every advanced catechism—or catechism of perseverance, as it is called—contains an abridgment of theology. It is unthinkable that a pious person, charged with the instruction of the young in the principles and truths of religion, should be without a sufficiently extensive knowledge of religion. Even in what concerns personal perfection, how can the soul be ignorant of religious truths which ought to be the daily food of its interior life.

In this matter we have met with much ignorance, which, though there were many extenuating circumstances to excuse it, was none the less deplorable. For example, we have often asked the question: " Why is God our Father and how are we His children? "—to receive answers which are inaccurate or insufficient. The answer most often given is—because we have been created by God. We have even met with souls who maintained that they were very happy to be able to attain to sanctity without being able to answer such a question: to whom we answer that St. Paul, instructing the first Christians, who were for the most part very simple and unlettered, thought it his duty to explain how they became the brothers of Jesus Christ and children of God, this truth being one of the corner-stones of Christianity and therefore most rich in spiritual significance.

In this doctrinal matter, we meet again the dangerous

illusion that the graces of prayer dispense from the duty of knowing and studying the truths which essentially constitute Catholic doctrine. We cannot understand how educated and observant minds can maintain that the great Christian mystics were little concerned with tradition. They obeyed their own dictates alone, it is said, even while seemingly obeying those of their confessor; their relations with God were so intense that they did not hesitate, when necessary, to ignore the authority of their director and to avail themselves of a superior liberty. The great fear of the true mystics, on the contrary, was the following of their own will and the failure thereby to continue the traditional redemptory work of Christ.

Except in very rare cases, the mystic who claims superior liberty in virtue of intuitions or revelations direct from God, is a heretic. It will suffice to re-read attentively the biographies and the works of St. Teresa, St. Jeanne de Chantal, St. Margaret Mary, to be convinced of this. St. Thérèse of the Child Jesus did not dare to give herself over to her way of confidence and of spiritual infancy until a priest assured her categorically that it was conformable to the teachings of the Gospel. It is absolutely false, however, that this obedience, this renouncing of self, this " disappropriation," destroys true initiative.

It is amazing to notice how, in spite of the fact that our doctors and our spiritual writers have many times refuted the error, some enlightened minds to-day still believe that the obedience and docility of a soul to divine teaching communicated by a director are incompatible with profound originality. Secular writers, even those who are most sympathetic to Catholicism, seem always to have the underlying conviction that in order to have a striking personality one must know how to refuse to obey and must zealously, guard a spirit of independence, even (and especially) when one has submitted to a director. St. Thomas clearly teaches, on the contrary, that the more one obeys God in the person of those who represent Him, by so much the more is one free. An analogous teaching is found in Pascal. The more a mystical soul is obedient and docile under the hand of God, by so much the more is it free and by so much has it enriched its true personality. All our spiritual writers and our doctors, without exception, teach that a profound emptying of oneself before God and His representatives, is the commencement of the work of the Holy Spirit within us and the renewing of the face of the earth.

We insist on the necessity of obedience because without it, souls who are determined to walk in the ways of holiness, infallibly err. Indeed, it is a necessary condition, that the soul should submit itself to the direction of a firm and enlightened guide. St. John of the Cross is very insistent on this. " Divine providence," he writes, " has ordained that men should be governed by men, and has made no exception in the matter of supernatural communications. His absolute wish is that we should withhold full assent to such unless they are approved by His authorized representatives, and thus every time He inspires a soul or reveals some knowledge to it, He also implants the desire to take counsel on the matter. We should always, then, accept the advice and direction of the Church and her ministers. *Vae soli*—woe to those who act by themselves alone. Before coming to a decision, the lone soul ordinarily feels feeble and uncertain, even though the idea has come to it from God. I, therefore, conclude: everything which the soul receives, in any supernatural manner whatsoever, ought to be communicated immediately, simply, fully, confidently, to his Spiritual Director." (Montée, xi, 3, Chap. XX.) Such is the teaching of the great mystical Doctor who can certainly not be accused of being lacking either in originality or in personality.

St. Teresa is equally explicit. " When God commands certain things or reveals the future, the soul must declare all to a prudent and experienced confessor, and neither act nor believe otherwise than as he directs." St. Teresa goes on to say that a refusal to do so is a proof that the revelations come from the devil or from serious nervous disorder.

Absolute submission to a lawful representative of the Church is not, then, as is so often said, an innovation, of St. Ignatius and his sons. The same principles of obedience are found with St. Francis de Sales and St. Vincent de Paul. Souls who enter on the way of perfection, ought to seek an enlightened spiritual guide. " Our Saviour," says St. Teresa, " will give light to His minister, or He will so arrange things that the soul cannot err in obeying him. There is no danger in acting thus, but the contrary course is full of peril."

We are perfectly aware—it is, indeed, one of the elementary truths insisted on from the beginning by our professors of moral theology—that a director ought to be careful not to allow himself to be led, unconsciously, by souls who seem to submit in a most docile manner to his direction. The case can occur frequently enough, especially when it is not question of a single soul, but of a collectivity, a community imbued with a special type of spirituality, or pushing to excess their attachment to a particular doctrine. It may happen, in such a case, that the confessor allows himself to be influenced and little by little the anomaly of the sheep leading the shepherd comes about. Such a situation is dangerous, because he is no longer acting as the legitimate authority who teaches the traditional and orthodox doctrine to souls called to perfection, and who guards it from the additions or subtractions to which even fervour can expose it.

When, for instance, spiritual souls are tempted to neglect, in the name of special graces received in prayer, the study of their religion or of the constitutions to which they are bound by their vows, it is the duty of the confessor to admonish these souls of their error, because members of a congregation or community ought to know to what they bind themselves in pronouncing simple, perpetual or solemn vows; they should also know all the articles of any importance in their rules, since the first condition of sanctification in a religious Order is the knowledge of its laws. Again we may seem to be labouring the obvious, but the negligence in this matter is often very astonishing.

It is indispensable that a soul destined for the life of perfection, should be familiar with certain characteristics of the spiritual life. To achieve this, it is not necessary to read many different books; it suffices that we choose an approved work and sound the depths of its teaching by careful reading. Soeur Thérèse, meeting her sister Céline in the library, confided to her: " I would have been ill-advised to have read all the books, for thus I should have lost precious time which I could have consecrated simply to loving God." But the saint had studied and re-read the *Imitation* so often in her youth that she knew it by heart, and could repeat an entire chapter when given its opening phrase. Later, when she had entered the Convent and was nearly eighteen years old, she read much in the treatises of St. John of the Cross. She read other books too, especially the lives of the saints. It is with astonishment that one meets in her work very characteristic thoughts borrowed from Blessed Henry Suso, from Tauler, from Mme. Swetchine and others. On analysis, therefore, her conduct and practice certainly do not authorize the neglect of reading. On her deathbed, she asked that they should read to her from the life of a saint. They thought to entertain her with stories of St. Francis and the birds, but she said: " No, find some examples of humility for me." It is certain that, had Soeur Thérèse lived long, she would have continued to search in pious works for examples and teaching concerning the virtues. She practised the counsel happily expressed by St. Francis de Sales, that we must read always in order to keep oil in the lamp of divine love, so that it may never burn low and die.

Some souls will object that the Gospel is sufficient for them, and that they have no need to draw from secondary sources, when they have therein the direct teaching of the Source Himself. We answer that it would be a grave error to suppose that it suffices to open the Gospel, select a passage and read it with self-sufficiency which dispenses with all other books and all commentaries. Nothing could be so dangerous as interpretations of the Gospel which are too personal, or an exclusive preference given to a certain number of fully concordant passages. When Tolstoy reached his last conversion and returned to the God of the Christian religion, he began to read again the Gospel of his childhood. As he read the text he underlined in red or blue certain words of Christ. He later advised his disciples to do the same, and to retain only the words thus chosen.

Pious souls do not, of course, deliberately adopt this method of exclusion, but they read by choice those thoughts in the Bible or the Gospel which they find most agreeable. Need we add that they interpret them in their own way too. It is astonishing to what illusions and to what excesses such conduct can lead. Many heresies have arisen from a unilateral interpretation, absolute or exclusive, of certain Gospel passages. A text in point is the saying of Our Saviour: " The hour cometh and now is when the true adorers shall adore the Father in spirit and in truth, for the Father seeketh such to adore him. God is a spirit, and they that adore him must adore him in spirit and in truth." (John IV, 23–24.) The conclusion has been drawn from this that there is no need for temples or churches. We have met some souls who have considerably shortened their vocal prayers and entirely abandoned the Rosary, because of the text: " When you pray, do not speak many words, as the heathens do: for they think that in their much-speaking they shall be heard." (Matt. VI, 7.) Persons who have received a careful religious education in a good Catholic family are instinctively guarded from such illusions, but, though they probably know and appreciate it little enough, they owe this to theologians and doctors who have long fought, even at the peril of their lives, to maintain a traditional and orthodox interpretation of the Gospel. The Gospel, in fact, must be known in its entirety to be properly understood, and, in the last analysis, the Church, which has received the deposit of faith, is alone qualified to fix the sense of disputed texts.

In our day, the need for taking steps against ignorance in Christian circles, has led to the institution of examinations in religious knowledge. Young girls who enter teaching Congregations often have a knowledge of the ancient languages and of the history of the Church. During their noviciate, they may even perfect their Latin and learn to translate the Scripture and particularly the Psalms and liturgical prayers. Some may even attempt the *Summa* with the aid of a translation. The criticism will be levelled at these, that there is no need to know so many things, that they may even be a hindrance to perfection and self-sanctification. It is true that even contemplation can easily degenerate, as a result of intellectual curiosity, into mere speculation. But the abuses into which it is always so easy to fall, cannot be quoted in condemnation of a legitimate use of study which prepares our minds for the better understanding of our religion.

To oppose such perfectly justifiable innovations because they are different from ancient custom and routine habits; to criticize all that is new because " all that has never been done before," is to adopt an obscurantist attitude— to mark time, refuse to advance, deny consciously or unconsciously the whole idea of progress. St. Madeleine Barat wrote: " It is weakness of spirit that makes one keep to the one routine through fear of change." A soul can certainly become very holy without acquiring great knowledge; but a congregation, an important religious community cannot fulfil its full apostolic mission, if it does not possess an *élite* with sufficient general culture. One of the saintly representatives of the first Franciscan generation having put the question to St. Bonaventure: " Could one become a saint without studying theology? " The holy Doctor replied: " Yes." The disciple departed, crying out joyfully: " Fra Bonaventure says that one can be a saint without studying theology." That was certainly true; but if the whole fraternity of Franciscans had been dispensed from study, the Order would never have fulfilled its destiny. The necessity of intellectual and especially of religious culture is particularly acute in our day, when numbers of young men and women are giving themselves to secondary studies. But without taking the point of view of the active apostolate, and by considering only the interior and contemplative life, there is still a necessity for some study of the Christian religion. We are perfectly aware that mystical souls have brooded long over the same mystery and, through the inspiration of the Holy Ghost, have profoundly sounded its depths; but, except in very rare cases, souls will find it of great advantage to meditate successively on the Christian mysteries. St. Teresa seems even severe on this matter: " Why," she asks, " when we have the infinite nature of God for our meditations, should we confine ourselves to one of His attributes alone." It sometimes happens that souls complain of suffering from a certain spiritual stagnation. On a little questioning, it is found that such souls persist in considering the same mystery, in practising the same devotion, and thereby never renew their interior life. From all these observations we draw the general conclusion that sanctification supposes a culture of soul more profoundly than is generally supposed; and that is so, whether one's viewpoint is that of the Apostolate or of individual perfection. The Curé d'Ars was regarded as very ignorant, and, while his fellow students in the Seminary held him in high esteem for virtue, they looked down on him a little for his little Latin and less Greek; yet those who later knew him intimately were amazed a his judgment, his extensive and exact religious knowledge, his real originality of thought. An even more ignorant saint, St. Joan of Arc, who could not even read, astonished the most subtle doctors of the University by the truth and the aptness of her answers.

Similar discoveries can be made about saints who were apparently very ignorant, when their character is more closely analysed. In default of prolonged study, they have observed much, they have interested themselves in all the moral and religious questions that they heard discussed, either in conversation or in sermons. They have remembered and meditated interiorly facts concerning

7

Jesus, the Blessed Virgin, the Apostles, martyrs and saints; their souls have become broken earth to all the good seed that falls. The Divine Genius—the Holy Ghost—Who directs by His gifts and graces, the development of virtues in the saints, has also, in a mysterious and often amazing way, formed their intelligence and their judgment. If they seem to have little of that knowledge, often superficial indeed, by means of which one can glitter in conversation, the saints are rich in profound and eternal truths. It was said of St. Thérèse of the Child Jesus at the process of her canonization: " You had to pay very great attention before you saw that she was very intelligent." It is true that Soeur Thérèse was completely and deliberately disinterested in all that is transitory, for her spirit was alive to supernatural truths alone. It was a similar lack of interest in the events of his day that made his brethren accuse St. John of the Cross of having a subnormal intelligence; but it suffices to go back half a century to recognize how often that lack of curiosity in passing events and so-called questions of the day, was abundantly fruitful. This indifference allowed them to be absorbed in meditation and contemplation of divine realities. All the souls who have undertaken, with the help of grace, the study of self necessary for the correction of faults, and who have laboured to imitate the virtues and the life of Our Lord, have acquired a profound knowledge of man, of his duties and his ends. This science of infinite value is the science of the saints.

CHAPTER SIX

*The Unsuspected Importance of Religious Art in the
Christian Life and Apostolate*

ASTONISHMENT may be the first reaction of many devout
souls to our decision to treat of religious art in a little
book with spiritual rebirth and sancity as its subject.
Those who feel inclined to skip this chapter should give a
moment's thought to the concern of the Christian Church
for art, from the catacomb years to our own day. If we
are monks or enclosed nuns, or belong to an Order or
monastic Congregation, or to a pious association, or if
our devotion leads us to aid our priests by ornamenting
their churches and altars, or if we take part in liturgical
ceremonies and chant—in all these cases, we necessarily
occupy ourselves with religious art. And this art has
always contributed greatly to the converting and sanctifying influence of our religion.

We recall, in this connection, the profound impression
made on St. Augustine, while he was still a Manichaean,
by the chanting of the faithful and the liturgical ceremonies
in the church of Milan. That impression contributed to
draw his soul to the faith. So many ceremonies and
religious gestures have become so familiar to us that we
do not even suspect their value. If one would take the
trouble to study in general and down to the least details,
the importance which religious art formerly played in

the ceremonies—for example in our public processions for the Feast of Corpus Christi—the subject would assume a much greater importance. Processions have not entirely disappeared, and there are other equivalents in our churches, so that, by confining our observation to the least attitudes of a truly believing assembly during a religious ceremony, we will find them profoundly impregnated with religious art.

If we pay attention, from this point of view, to our least gestures, to the sacred words, to the prayers which we recite, to the signs of the cross, to the genuflections and inclinations and different traditional attitudes which we observe during the holy Sacrifice of the Mass and at Benediction, we shall again remark the importance which Christianity, wise in its knowledge of man's nature and of the mysteries it wishes to inculcate, has attached to religious art. A very fervent priest, a saint, by his manner of reciting public prayers, of genuflecting, or prostration, of chanting, of attention to the least rubrics, practises excellently, though he may not be conscious of it, religious art. When the Curé of Ars celebrated Mass, he took care to observe rigorously all the rites, all the gestures prescribed by the Canon. " Without the least appearance of distraction, his external movements seemed the outward expression of what passed within his soul. An enemy to all affectation, he exaggerated none of his gestures, and added none; but his eyes, now raised, now lowered, prayed; his hands, joined or extended, made supplication. A silent preaching of great eloquence." (Trochu, p. 382.)

When it is appreciated that the prayers of the Mass— their beauty and variety, the short and repeated dialogue with the server, the invocations successively addressed to the saints, to Our Saviour, to God the Father, to the Holy Trinity—make, so to speak, a sacred poem of simple and divine sublimity, it is easy to understand that the priest who, without being a Curé d'Ars, celebrates Mass piously, reverently, and religiously, performs a work which is not only of infinite value, but also of incomparable aesthetic worth.[1] Unbelievers are often more moved by the exterior beauty of the Offices than are the faithful who are accustomed to seeing them. When it is not the priest only, but the whole congregation which prays, stands at the Gospel, genuflects, prostrates at the Elevation—in a word, when priest and congregation are intimately united in offering the Holy Sacrifice, then indeed, as we said above, it becomes a sermon of great beauty and supernatural eloquence.

If Christians, priests and faithful, appreciated at their true grandeur the traditional and actual importance of their Offices, they would draw greater fruits from them for their own souls, and would have at heart to increase their edifying power. Since the last century, great efforts have been made to increase the honour given to Christian Liturgy and to perfect the execution of the chants which it contains. Nevertheless, even in pious associations and religious communities, how many faults could be corrected in a short time, by an enlightened piety, truly interior and guided by good taste! We freely admit that certain nuns, for special and very serious reasons, have not adopted the chant of the different parts of the Mass, nor that of the psalms and hymns which is customary at Benediction;

[1] As I translate these words, an article on " the Theatre and Catholic Values " has appeared in the *Catholic Herald* for March 25th, 1949, from the powerful pen of Paul Vincent Carroll. He says: " It is, I think, significant that Catholicism is in itself theatrical in the very highest sense of the word. The Confessional is a stage shrouded in sombre curtains of tragedy, with one divine spotlight; the Stations of the Cross are an episodic drama of overwhelming emotions; the Blessed Eucharist is a sublime and flawless poem; the Holy Mass is the greatest Classical drama that ever was written."
TRANSLATOR'S NOTE.

in all cases, we much prefer psalmody to bad chant, but such psalmody should be sweet, smooth, harmonious and pious. It is too easily taken for granted that good psalmody can be obtained without much practice. Much preparation and practice *is* necessary; and for the plain chant of the different parts of the Mass, if the execution is to be satisfactory, practice is absolutely necessary. Piety itself and a true religious sense will cause pious souls to avoid all negligence in this matter. No priest or monk, whose actions are guided by a profound interior life, will recite the Psalms, or celebrate Mass, or chant it with lightness and indifference; and the same can be said, in their measure, of the pious faithful who participate in the chants and the ceremonies of the Church. A sincerely Christian soul is too deeply penetrated with the importance of his duties, the grace which he can receive and the edification he can give, the apostolate he can exercise on such occasions, to allow himself to be negligent or to assume distracted or thoughtless attitudes.

It is regrettable sometimes, when assisting at religious offices in public churches or even in community chapels, to notice how, with less trouble but with a little more docility to the traditional directive of the Church, faults could be avoided which mar the beauty of the divine cult. We have often alluded to Church tradition. The truly Christian tradition, while always counselling prayer in common, has favoured also the chant of the faithful. " When two or three are gathered together in my name, I am in the midst of them." (Matt. xviii, 20.) The Christian sense of fraternity and community causes souls intimately united with Christ, to desire that all should participate as much as possible in the prayers addressed to God, to the Blessed Virgin and to the saints. The first Christians did not listen, with more concern for beauty of voice than for praise of God, to a singer or group of singers. Sometimes the celebrant is forced to recite the prayers of the Canon in a loud voice to avoid error, and pious souls are completely distracted, by choral per- formances which are more suited to theatre than church, being simply a menace to recollection and prayer. We shall not go into further detail: it will suffice to say that in all that concerns the liturgical ceremonies and the divine cult, we should take care to avoid all profane art and, in general, all that is not inspired by truly religious sentiment. We think that this, in our world especially, is an indispensable condition of spiritual renaissance.

What has been said should suffice to show us that art, in the wide sense of the word, has an importance in the Christian religion, which is often unsuspected. Imagine an ancient pagan returned to earth and visiting our towns and villages. He is astonished to find in each an edifice, topped by tower or steeple, dominating town and village. Entering one such, he is amazed still more by the stained glass, the great crucifix, benches, altars, pictures, statues, tribune: and turning, he will immediately ask if he has entered a public building devoted to the teaching of moral, aesthetic and religious doctrine. So far, we feel, our hypothetical pagan. . . . But the majority of actual Christians scarcely recognize that our churches, or chapels, from those in our monasteries to the least of our villages, have been the first centres of civilization where our ancestors have learned the mysteries and the beauty of our religion.

The Curé of Ars received no artistic training, and, had he remained in his family absorbed by the work of the fields, he would certainly never have been concerned to capture the regard and simple admiration of his fellow workers. But, called to the priesthood and appointed

Curé of a very lax village, he quickly saw the necessity to beautify and enlarge his church in order to attract his parishioners. It is thus that the humble and unlettered Curé began, according to his ability, to practise the rudiments of Christian art. Almost immediately on his arrival, he restored the high altar, decorating and painting it himself. Successively, he added five chapels to his church, built a tower, enlarged the entrance. The poor Curé, filled with zeal, indulged big ideas. He wrote to the Mayor: " I want the approach to the Church to be very beautiful. This is very necessary, because, if the palaces of earthly kings have magnificent approaches, how much more so ought the approach to our churches be sumptuous . . ." It was apostolic care alone which suggested to this priest, who was considered the least Curé in the diocese, the project of a church which would be comparable in magnificence to the palace of a king.

" It sometimes requires only the sight of an image," he said in one of his sermons, " to touch and convert us." His biographer, Trochu, has told of his delight in the beautiful statues he acquired, and how he wept before *Ecce Homo*. " There is a little curé who wanders around our shops," said the furniture-dealers and jewellers of Lyon, " thin and frailly built, with every appearance of not having a sou in his pocket, and yet wanting only the very best for his church."

We have dwelt on the case of the Curé d'Ars because it is a very typical example of how traditional Christian piety, always apostolic, leads souls inevitably to use images, statues, ornaments and all the relevant things in the domain of art.

This truth is strikingly borne out by the history of the first years of devotion to the Sacred Heart. Having communicated, by dint of submission and perseverance, her cult of the Sacred Heart to the Visitandines about her, St. Margaret Mary sought for an image which would arrest the eye and move the heart, since such an image was necessary if the devotion was to become popular. Mère Greyfie, converted to the devotion after having strenuously opposed it, painted a picture in oils representing the Heart of Jesus. Soon, St. Margaret was distributing large numbers of these images of the Sacred Heart in every home. About the same time, the first chapel dedicated to the Sacred Heart was erected at Paray-le-Monial, and soon every convent of the Visitation built one. It was thus that a Visitandine, eminently contemplative and desiring above all to remain hidden and forgotten, became unconsciously the initiator of a devotion destined to inspire many paintings, sculptures, churches and basilicas.

In our own day, we have witnessed a phenomenon not less wonderful. The humble Carmelite nun who lived totally forgotten, caused, immediately after her death, a religious movement which soon expressed itself in images, statues, and artistic objects of every kind, in all parts of the Christian world. It was popular piety which required countless pictures of Soeur Thérèse; which wished to possess, even before her canonization, souvenirs and little relics of the saint; which inaugurated pilgrimages of such dimensions that the modest little chapel had to be enlarged, and would finally become a basilica. So true is it, that the Spirit breatheth where He listeth, and that a completely hidden and intense spiritual life can clothe itself in the forms of sensible things to spread to the whole world. Fifty years ago, the good Religious of Carmel would have been stupefied and bewildered had someone foretold the numberless works and crushing responsibilities which they had soon to face. Doubtless, we are not destined to a like task; nevertheless, we should meditate seriously on the duty of a Christian generation to assure the artistic continuity of tradition.

All the achievements of beauty in Church tradition can form a treasury which ought to be guarded and handed on by the Christian *élite* of every generation. Many monuments of religious art can of themselves last for centuries; but it is the duty of successive generations to bequeath to their children the knowledge of these monuments. Now, history shows that there has been grave neglect in this matter in certain epochs. Thus, for example, there were periods when the grandeur of art in the first centuries, and the sublimity of our Gothic cathedrals, and the lofty inspiration and conscientious execution in so many admirable masterpieces, were far from being properly appreciated. It is a very short time ago, indeed, when there was no taste for liturgy and all that it implies— Church hymns, Gregorian chant, etc. Events independent of human control, wars and public calamities, have often been the point of departure for these interruptions in tradition and the neglect they entail; but, in spite of extenuating circumstances, the chief cause remains a certain deficiency in the virtue of religion and in Christian sentiment. We should remember the words of Huysmans: " Ugliness has a necessary relation to the devil, for it reflects him, as beauty reflects God." That is summary and over-simplified, but it contains a great amount of truth. Many secondary causes can engender ugliness, and we cannot demand of fervent souls, even of saints, that they should be always creators and inspirers of beauty.

Mgr. Bougaud remarks: " that after two centuries of gropings and of trials, we still await the master who will breathe on the canvas, in the immaterial beauty of the passion which devours It, the adorable Heart of Jesus

Christ." He recalls that the early Christians attempted to paint in the catacombs the qualities of Our Saviour, of the Blessed Virgin and the Apostles. " The art in these pictures," he says, " is often nil, but there is soul in them." One can hardly expect much more from Christians of any age; real masterpieces are rare, and those which represent Christ and the Saints are easily counted. We are not to be held responsible, of course, for the fact that a statue of the Sacred Heart or of Soeur Thérèse is not a work of genius. We have the right to require only that pious souls who are drawn to the painting of religious subjects should exclude all vanity, all profane inspiration, and express only faith, charity, and supernatural sentiments.

It frequently happens that, in the construction and decorating of churches, the temptation to search for what pleases by provoking a superficial and too human admiration, is too easily indulged. If the motives behind such building are analysed, it will be found that some are unworthy because they rest on sentiments which are not as profound or as purely Christian as they should be. Some of the vanity and secret pride which can never be completely banished from the human heart, mix with our zeal. In this sense, ugliness, according to Huysmans, comes very often, if not always, from sin or from the devil.

The remark attributed to an Athenian before a statue sculptured by a foreign artist, deserves to be immortal: " You have made it rich because you are unable to make it beautiful." Many zealous Christians err in thinking that they have erected churches, convents and monuments of great artistic and religious worth, because they have spent a great deal of money on them. It is significant that the saintly reformers of religious Orders met with great opposition to their ideas of religious architecture. The nakedness and austerity of the churches and monasteries constructed by the first Cistercians in the twelfth century under the inspiration of St. Bernard, contrasts sharply with the magnificence and luxury of the churches and cloisters built by the Monks of Cluny; but the Cistercian reform had scarcely any enduring influence. Less than a century later, the Founders of the Mendicant Orders, St. Francis and St. Dominic, were opposed with all their might to monumental buildings. St. Dominic, returning to the monastery of Bologne after some months of absence, found that Fra Bonvisi, the procurator, had commenced the building of some foundations. Weeping, the saint accused his Brethren of desiring to possess rich houses, and gave orders that the work should cease. Immediately after his death, the work was enthusiastically recommenced. St. Francis was even more severe on Fra Pierre de Stacia, who proposed to found a house of studies and a fine monastery at Bologne, for he ordered him to desist, and when Fra Pierre proved obstinate in his idea, he cursed it. The same cult of poverty is found with St. Teresa. " Let poverty be strictly observed," she writes, " for it will be a much stronger rampart than magnificence of buildings. Be careful, my daughters, never to build superb edifices—this I beg of you for the love of God and by the precious Blood of His Son. If you build such, my prayer is that it collapse the very day it is erected. It would be a great evil, my daughters, to build great houses with the money of the poor. I beg Our Saviour to preserve you from it."

All the reformers, in different ways, have professed the same teaching. If, urged by an ardent zeal for religious perfection, they seem to us to have sometimes pushed to excess the cult of poverty, it is because they have realized how powerful is the hereditary instinct in man to construct and possess, and how that almost irresistible tendency is contrary to Christian perfection. St. Francis de Sales himself, the saint of the golden mean, would not allow an episcopal palace to be built for his own use; he could easily have done so, for there were many benefactors, but he refused, saying that he was only too happy to resemble Our Saviour in not having a house to call his own.

The admonitions and the heroic example given and practised by those whom the church has canonized and proposed as our models, have not always been followed to the letter. The absolute poverty practised by Jesus and his apostles, by St. Francis, St. Dominic, St. Teresa and their first followers, has not been observed in the Church except temporarily, and little by little the practice of collective ownership has been reverted to. For many reasons, of which some are very legitimate, we cannot dispense ourselves, as St. Bernard and St. Francis would have desired, from building beautiful churches and great convents, but we must guard constantly against the human tendency to build too beautifully, too richly, with excessive decoration. For thus built, monastic houses lose their serious character; they do not preach by their very appearance the evangelical truths and virtues; and they are a subject of vanity and vain glory. *Nonne et ethnici hoc faciunt?*—Do not the unbelievers this?

At all times, men have had a passion for building. It seems that this passion could be often more inveterate in them than self-interest. We need not return to the tower of Babel to prove this. " The malady of building-stones " is a well-seasoned expression. In the thirteenth century, Pierre le Chantre denounced what he called the *morbus aedificandi*. The construction of a cathedral or church or monastery is an excellent work, *opus divinum*, which can engross a bishop or an abbot, so that he concerns himself much more with it than with the apostolate. This passion is native to every century, and, with the best of good faith, people are persuaded that they have fulfilled the mandate with which Providence has charged them, by being absorbed, during their whole life, in undertaking and completing such buildings. The *maître-de-l'oeuvre* or the architect thus becomes the true inspirer and animator of an abbey or community, and the work of God is relegated to the second place, just as though Christ had not said to all those who have the care of souls: " Go and teach all nations." Undoubtedly, it is difficult to build, but it is much more difficult still to build the house of the Holy Spirit in Christian souls. It is also true that it is more difficult to preserve intact and to develop religious observances and religious discipline than to maintain and develop houses.

We have no intention of censuring those who build legitimately to God's glory; we wish only to place them on their guard against the excesses into which they can be so easily drawn in this matter. Others have done so before us.

In the eleventh century, St. Bernard inveighs against great and rich monuments. " O vanity of vanities! O surpassing foolishness! The Church is resplendent in her walls and naked in her poor! Her stones are clothed with gold, her children are bare! With the money of the poor, the eyes of the rich are charmed! The curious have satisfaction, and the unfortunate have not wherewith to live." Let us leave to the great reformers their vigorous invectives. The excess to which we refer is so well known that there is no need to insist. We shall add just one further consideration.

Sometimes virtuous souls are met with who believe, in all good faith, that they practise the vow and cultivate the spirit of poverty in a perfect manner, because they deprive themselves of superfluities and even of necessities, in order that they may realize a sum necessary for the construction of an over-luxurious church or a vast and over-rich convent. We do not deny that, in certain conditions, the individual observance of the virtue of poverty can be very meritorious; but, in general, to work without respite, to pinch oneself with a rigid meanness, in order to accumulate superfluous riches, is often the very contrary to evangelical poverty. Care must be taken not to fall into the common error of the spirit of economy, which hoards, with the supernatural and perfect spirit of poverty. Christ counsels His Disciples and the rich young man, to go and sell all that they have, in order that they may be free of all temporal worries and consecrate themselves to prayer, to the spiritual life, to the apostolate. St. Francis, St. Dominic, St. Teresa did precisely that, in imitation of the Divine Master.

We have already remarked that the absolute detachment counselled by Our Saviour cannot be observed by the great majority of Christians, nor even by all those who officially have charge of souls. It may be objected that religious art supposes a certain amount of wealth, and—in the large sense—of luxury, even. The artist will ask whether we propose to suppress what are called the treasures of the ancient churches. We answer that, so far from such being our proposal, our view is, on the contrary, probably much larger than the objector's, in what concerns the sculptures and the paintings of our churches. As priests and apostles, we consider, before all else, the salvation of souls; so that, in choosing statues and images, we take, first and foremost, the point of view of the interest and edification which they cause to the faithful. Purely artistic considerations take second place. The important thing is that such statues and pictures should

capture the imagination, should stir the minds and souls
of the faithful, in order to entice them into our churches
where they will hear eternal truths. The horizon of
Christian charity is incomparably more extensive than
that of purely aesthetic beauty.

A well-intentioned critic has observed, for example,
that the strength and austerity of a certain famous
sanctuary of pilgrimage to-day, can be appreciated after
the sweet and attractive that satisfied before: but we have
personal experience that the people are never attracted
in this way. For if the multitudes had not first taken,
little by little, the unbeaten track of this pilgrimage, the
theologians would not have been drawn to examine the
religious questions involved, and the aesthetes and artistic
amateurs would not have come to sharpen their tools on
us.

The fact is, that if we wish to form the Christian people
to an appreciation of religious art, we must adapt that art
to them, such as they are, in order to lift them by successive
stages to the understanding of works of greater worth.
A provincial Curé is sometimes limited in his choice to
coloured and even somewhat defective statues, because
they are the kind that attract his parishioners to prayer;
and to attract to goodness and prayer is the point of view
from which the Curé views the whole matter—a point of
view which is foreign to the artistic amateur. We would
unhesitatingly follow the example of St. Francis De Sales
who, because it was a means of gaining souls, spoke to the
Chablais peasants in a patois of Italian and French; we
would break all the rules in the grammar if by doing so
we could gain souls. If our people to-day have lost the
appreciation of stained glass, of statues, of artistic religious
sculpture, which characterized our ancestors of the mighty
thirteenth century, we can but bitterly regret it. But,

without losing time in long analyses of the causes of this slump in taste, we must busy ourselves with putting before the people what *is* within their powers of appreciation. We shall, of course, endeavour to cultivate their taste, and to raise it, little by little, to an appreciation of high and supernatural beauty.

The *spiritual renaissance*, which we are happy to notice in our age, will, if at all stable, necessarily entail a corresponding progress in the domain of Christian art; but such progress demands the existence and action of an *élite* who, that they may let their light shine by doctrine and by art, sit down to learn at the feet of the saints.

Part Three

THE UNITIVE LIFE

Chapter Seven

NECESSARY AND PROVIDENTIAL TRIALS

S<small>T. THÉRSÈ</small> of the Child Jesus writes in her autobiography: "I did not think that much suffering must
be endured in order that a soul may attain to holiness, but
the good God soon revealed this to me through many
trials." She also declared that she was not a single day
without having something to suffer or to combat, and she
asked her sisters, on her deathbed, to make this fact known
to souls after her death, in order, she said, "that the
authenticity of her mission should be consecrated with the
mark of the cross."

In making this request, Soeur Thérèse continued, even
while she renewed, the Christian tradition. Those who
think that they can attain to sanctity without suffering
much, greatly err. It can, of course, be said that Soeur
Thérèse made suffering lovable, but for all that, she did
not abolish it. Many centuries before, in a sentence which
has become proverbial, St. Augustine said: "Where
love is, there is no labour, or if there is, the labour is
loved." This truth is immediately applicable to suffering;
love does not cause it to disappear. The trials of the just
and, above all, of the soul which desires to attain to holiness
will always be countless: *multae tribulationes justorum.*

Souls whom God wishes to sanctify pass through trials
of every kind, lasting often throughout their entire lives.

One of the most characteristic truths of the doctrine of St. John of the Cross is that a soul may inflict the most painful mortifications on itself and not attain to sanctity, if God, with His own hand, does not try that soul or permit it to be cruelly tried. Voluntarily imposed suffering has not the same profoundly purifying power as have heaven-sent trials, passively borne in a spirit of resignation; nor have they the same meritorious value. The trials sent or permitted by providence should reach and purify the innermost recesses of our hearts, like the red-hot knife which a kind, but apparently pitiless hand presses into the flesh and even into the marrow of the bone.

The first and most common of trials is that of physical suffering. If we have not experienced very severe maladies, we are unconsciously inclined to diminish their importance. We do not go so far as to assert, with one of the most delicate and most penetrating of the writers of the last century, that, all things considered, physical suffering with its tortures is what man dreads most. It is true that bodily suffering, when it is continuous and very severe, becomes, even for the most energetic characters, humanly insupportable. Moreover, when it has attained its height, it always brings moral trials in its train: temptations to discouragement, to despair, to doubt the goodness of God. Soeur Thérèse knew these very dark hours in her last illness. She said one morning: "Ma mère, if you could know what I suffer! Pray for me. Ah! you would really need to experience it to know what it is like. Be careful, when you have invalids in the grip of violent depression, to leave no poison near them. When suffering is at its height, it requires very little to cause the loss of reason." All the saints have not, perhaps, known this excess of suffering: nevertheless, when their lives are read with some attention, it is found that there are scarcely any who, in their youth or maturity, have not been cruelly tried by sickness. Examples are easily to hand. St. Bernard, from the age of thirty, was afflicted with very grave stomach trouble. St. Teresa of Avila, in the first year of her life in Carmel, was seized with such violent heart-attacks that she frightened her Sisters. Her condition was made worse by a patent course of treatment which she followed. " The sufferings which I endured in my heart," she wrote, " were so intense that sometimes I seemed to be torn asunder with pointed teeth. They reached such a pitch of intensity that I thought I should go mad." She had to be lifted in a sheet, for she could not endure the contact of a hand. St. Francis de Sales, who was less tried, suffered " a severe and long malady " when he was nearly thirty. The sufferings of the Curé d'Ars—facial neuralgia, awful toothache, severe internal torture—are appalling. Yet, in spite of them, he spent only three hours of the twenty-four in bed. His sufferings often kept him awake, and then he lighted his candle in order to contemplate the images of the saints in his room. " Often," it has been reported of him, " he was so tired on returning to his house that he could scarcely mount the stairs. I have seen him fall against the wall." Nevertheless, to use the words of the Countess des Garets, " he got through work which would have exhausted six confessors."

Although of a robust constitution, St. Vincent de Paul suffered during his whole life from many maladies. He frequently visited the Hospital of Saint-Lazare, and he would comfort the sick with the words: " Do not fear, brother, I have had this infirmity in my youth and I have been cured. . . . Be patient: there is still reason to hope that your sickness will pass, and that God wills to achieve something more through you."

Such examples could be multiplied, to show that physical suffering, when a person knows how to profit by it, is one of the most precious schools of holiness through which the saints have passed. It has taught them to count only on the help of God, and to live supernaturally and, in a sense, miraculously. While adopting an exclusively natural and even pagan point of view, certain philosophers who have studied deeply the psychology of man, have been quite alive to the marvellous power of suffering. " I desire for those whom I in any way regard," writes Nietzsche, " that they should meet with suffering, abandonment, sickness. . . . I do not offer them my pity, for I wish them the only thing that can show, to-day, whether a man has any value or not. . . ." But what Pascal said of Epictetus can be applied to Nietzsche: he is " one of those philosophers of the world who has best known the duties of man. . . . I venture to say that he deserved to be worshipped, had he but known his weakness, since he must needs be God to know any man. So, as he was but earth and ashes, after having well understood what man ought . . . he lost himself in presuming to say what man is able to do."

The saints have not doubted that it was possible for them to attain to a perfection which raised them above human nature, but they have believed and have laboured to become more and more convinced that they can do nothing of themselves and that their power is from the grace of Jesus Christ. Feeling themselves called to imitate him in all things and to perpetuate His Passion and His Redemption, they have learned that they cannot discharge their mission without suffering and patience.

This mission, as we have pointed out, supposes, first of all, physical sufferings, but it is composed, above all, of moral sufferings of every kind. From the point of view of facts and of experience, it is very difficult, if not impossible, to trace a systematic order in these sufferings. The succession of trials varies very much from one saint to another; some have met them in youth, others in maturity. Add to this, that it is sometimes difficult to determine if a particular trial is ordained to what is called the purification of the senses or the purification of the spirit.

St. Francis de Sales had to endure a grave moral temptation. It began as an insinuation and soon became an obsession—the whisper that he was not in the state of grace. His soul was deprived of all the consolations of divine love. He asked himself whether these drynesses and spiritual aridities were not the punishment of some grave infidelity or of some mortal sin; he began to reflect on the theory of the small number of the elect, on the deep mystery of predestination, on the rigour of the judgments of God: it seemed impossible that he should be of the number of the elect, not because grace was wanting to him, but because he was failing to measure up to grace. As nearly always happens, the moral trial soon brought on bodily sickness, " so that he could neither eat, nor drink, nor sleep." There was here, above all, a purifying of the spirit by suffering: the saint was then only seventeen, and the physical sufferings we refer to came much later.

Nevertheless, the purification of the senses normally precede those of the spirit, but we must not attempt to establish clear-cut distinctions and a rigid order. St. Thérèse of the Child Jesus experienced an obsessing temptation to gluttony, and was haunted by imaginings of rare and succulent dishes. These imaginings, which forced themselves upon her and which she resisted, ordinarily have to do with the purification of the senses; yet, the saint was then in the last weeks of her final malady. It is disconcerting, when one has studied theoretical treatises of ascetic and mystical doctrine, to meet such a trial in a saint already arrived at the stage of union and spiritual marriage. She confided to her sister, with a sigh: " To think that all my life it has been a penance to me to have to eat, and now I seem to be dying of hunger! Oh, how afraid I am to die of hunger, and how sunk I am in material things! Come quickly, my God, and seek for me." It was, indeed, an anticipation of her Purgatory for the saint, in order that her soul, on separating from its body, should be so pure as to pass immediately to Heaven.

We have said sufficient on this matter: it is much more important that we should go on to warn souls insufficiently familiar with spiritual teaching, against another error. Many readers of St. John of the Cross or of a commentary on his doctrine, almost inevitably get the idea that one must pass completely through the night of the senses, and only then the night of the spirit. Now, in most cases, it happens that souls who resolve to consecrate themselves to a more perfect life, experience the purifications of the senses, and very shortly afterwards, certain purifications of the spirit. In fact, the doctrine of St. John of the Cross is that the senses are not wholly purified, if the spirit is not also in great measure purified. He writes: " It is through the painful and hard purification of the spirit, that all the imperfections of the spiritual and the sensitive parts of the soul must disappear, because one can never be fully purified apart from the other, and the purity of the senses is not well advanced unless that of the spirit is perceptibly on the way to realization . . . for the imperfections and the disorders of the sensitive part have their roots in and draw their sap from the spirit."

In the solitude of Sarteano, St. Francis of Assisi, when he had embraced the most complete poverty and was leading a rigorous, contemplative, and very exalted life, was yet haunted by grave temptations. Now, these temptations were of the sensible order, for they urged him to renounce celibacy and to marry. In order to conquer these desires and to master his flesh, he inflicted a cruel flagellation on himself with the cord which served him as cincture, and finally rolled himself naked in the snow. This well-known episode in the life of St. Francis shows us how a person who has renounced all things and is already far advanced in the way of holiness can yet be obsessed with sensual temptations which are ordinarily met with only in the early stages of the spiritual life. We have spoken of the bodily sufferings which nearly always attend those who have seriously entered on the way of holiness; but it cannot be maintained that such physical trials are necessarily the first. They are ordinarily preceded by a struggle unto death with ourselves, with our appetites, with our passions, with repugnances of the spirit, indecisions of the will, doubts of the intellect. This struggle supposes alternating light and darkness, joy and sorrow, exaltation and depression, according to the celebrated law of the two contrary states, so well formulated by St. Ignatius of Loyola. It is seldom that a soul who aspires to high perfection escapes these states in the beginning. It is then, especially, that it behoves the soul to remember this rule of the *Exercises*: " Never change in the time of desolation the resolutions which one has made before falling into it: try to change only the interior dispositions, that is to say, the desolation itself."

Another trial will consist in contradiction from those who surround us. We speak not only to those souls who desire, either in the world or in religion, to give themselves to a pious, Christian life, but above all to those who aspire to raise themselves to holiness. It is these especially who will meet in the execution of their design, the most vexatious contradictions. St. Teresa of Avila was long content, in the Carmel of the Incarnation, with a moderately religious life, which saved her from any criticism. When, however, she decided to answer the call of God and to lead a more perfect life, she was straightway severely criticized by the very Sisters who till then had only praise and approval for her. Their disapproval became violent when she conceived and carried out the project of founding a little house where, with some companions, she could vow herself to a more austere and more contemplative life. Almost unanimously condemned, not only by the religious, but by the confessors whom she consulted, her only comfort was St. Peter of Alcantara. " This holy man," she writes, " was penetrated with the most lively compassion for me. He told me that one of the greatest trials possible was that which I had endured—contradiction from the good. He added that there was much yet to suffer, because there was nobody in Avila who understands me."

St. Thérèse of the Child Jesus had entered the Carmel of Lisieux with the firm intention of observing the Rule perfectly and in the smallest details. " From the beginning," says her Mistress of Novices, " the servant of God amazed the community by a bearing that had something of the majestic in it, and which one would be far from expecting in a child of fifteen." The T.R. Mère Agnes de Jésus, who had been the little mother of Thérèse, testifies: " The Sisters, who for the most part expected to see a very ordinary child, were filled with respect in her presence. There was in her whole person something so dignified, so firm, so modest, that I was myself surprised at it." But jealousy, so natural to man and the unsuspected source of so many sentiments and judgments, was not slow to raise its head among certain of her companions.

" Her extraordinary regularity," we are told, " appeared to some Sisters in Carmel as silent reproach, and they sometimes showed spite and jealousy." This *extraordinary regularity* had its reactions even in quite high places. By heredity and by nature, the T.R. Mère Marie de Gouzague then Prioress, was an imperious character with an appetite for domination. Such a character loves to be approved and flattered, but Soeur Thérèse was too nobly moulded to stoop to flattery. This partly explains why, from her entry in Carmel, the postulant was treated very severely by Mère Marie. " I could not meet her," writes Soeur Thérèse, " without also meeting with reproach."

Those who attempt, in an atmosphere of live-and-let-live, to practise a rigid, literal observance of the Rule, will meet with the same difficulty. If they lack energy, tenacity, and, above all, constancy in prayer, they will not persevere. Scarcely had St. John of the Cross noticed that the Rule was modified in the Carmel of Medina, than, anxious to answer the call to a solitary and austere life, he forced himself to live according to the primitive Rule. In spite of his humility and his desire to live unnoticed, St. John of the Cross, by force of circumstances, stood out. " When all parts move equally," says Pascal, " nothing appears to move, as in a ship. . . . He who stops becomes a fixed point, showing the movement of the others." However, in spite of opposition, St. John did not grow slack, and his superiors learned to appreciate his virtue no less than his application to study and to theology. When he became master of studies, he did not diminish his mortifications and prayers. Some of his brethren grew unable to support the silent lesson contained in his way of life. At his approach, they would say to one another: " Let us get out of this devil's way." St. John was then only twenty-five.

Henri Suso, after five years of relative ease in the Dominican Priory of Constance, felt a desire to come to grips with himself. He imposed a severe rule on himself and he preserved solitude and silence. One asked—"What strange manner of life is this you have adopted?" Another counselled that the ordinary was the safest life: and a third predicted an unhappy ending to it all. The young Religious suffered greatly from not having anyone in whom to confide, and he began sometimes to doubt his plans, so that he even returned at times to the conversations and useless distractions of his brethren. Such returns were followed by remorse of conscience, until he entered fully on the path of perfection, even though it cost him many trials and much suffering.

Sufficient has been said to show that the soul who enters resolutely on the road to sanctity, must expect the criticism of the lax and the lukewarm, certainly; but certainly, too, of those who practise a sincerely Christian and even holy life.

"Who then," writes Henri Joly, "is the founder or the reformer of an Order, the revealer of the beginner of a devotion destined to become universal, who has not had to suffer, I do not say from his enemies, but from his friends, his brethren, and his sisters in the faith." (*Psychologie des Saints*, p. 36.) Souls of the second order or who are not inspired by grace, are astonished and even scandalized by these oppositions; but the saints understand that it is good for them to be cruelly contradicted. When Br. Elias complained to St. Francis of the opposition he met with among the brethren, the saint replied: "You ought to regard it as a grace, when your brothers, too, as well as other men, are against you. You ought to wish it so and not otherwise, and it will thus become better for you than a retreat in a hermitage."

In meditating on the lives of the saints, one is amazed by the lack of understanding and the accusations they have met with from those who ought to have aided them most. That such opposition is one of the greatest trials of the saints, is proved by a famous saying of the Curé d'Ars. Anonymous, bitter letters, denouncing the Curé, had been received by his new Bishop, Mgr. Devic, and the latter thought it his duty to send the Curé of Trevoux to collect information on the conduct of M. Vianney. M. Trochu assures us that it was these incidents the Curé d'Ars had in mind when, towards the end of his life, he said: "Had I known when I arrived at Ars all that I must suffer, I would have died from the blow." There is a similar admission from St. John Baptist de la Salle. His whole life was filled with opposition and treason, so much so that he said these moving words to his most devoted benefactors, in his last years: "When God showed me the good that would be done by the Institute of Brothers, had He also revealed the crosses and the sufferings which must accompany it, my courage would have failed me, and I would not have dared to touch it with the tip of my finger."

The defection of early friends is the trial which seems to have touched most nearly the quick of the souls of the saints. The distressing cries of St. Bernard are well known, in which he pleads with Robert de Chatillon, a Religious whom he loved and who abandoned him to return to Cluny. The most tender and devoted affection, when it is not supernaturalized, cannot stand up to the inevitable suffering of the religious life. All the psychologists have underlined the dangers to which a too natural sympathy is exposed. "All love," says Henri Joly, "whatsoever its object and however sincere the heart from which it comes, has its changes, its waxings and its wanings. It can be over-exacting, over-jealous; it can demand more than its due, and fail to consider what it owes."

As gold, in the classical comparison, must be placed in the fire to be purified of all its alloy, so must the hearts of all those who aspire to perfection be passed through the crucible of suffering. Mère Barat, abandoned by some of her most dear daughters and opposed by others, accepted passively and in a supernatural spirit all the suffering entailed, but her health was so gravely shattered that many times she was thought to be on the point of death. At the same time she was tortured with the doubt that perhaps she was failing in her task, and that her own faults, which she magnified a hundredfold, was the cause of all the opposition to her and to her institute.

St. John Baptist de la Salle was ceaselessly attacked by the new Curé of Saint-Sulpice, was set aside, was replaced by another superior, was betrayed and ignominiously deceived by the Abbé Clement and by his friend M. Rogier. "A day or so after his condemnation," writes Blain, " he knew himself to be surrounded in Paris with open and secret persecutors, so that it was no longer safe to remain there. He fled and hid himself in Provence, without making known to anyone where he was, and even neglecting to reply to letters from his brothers." (Laudet —Vie, p. 114.) A careful examination of this saint's life, with its heap-up trials, reveals that he looked on himself as nothing. He hid himself and became a stranger to his own work for more than two years.

How many other saints there were, thus exiled from the work they had founded, ostracized by their own brethren, and in addition obsessed by anguished doubts as to the legitimacy of their own calling. St. John of the Cross wrote out of his own experience: " Trouble is always useless, for no good results from disturbance of soul.

Even if all should vanish and fade; if the course of events twists our purpose and sets it against us, more harm than good will come from trouble of soul. We must accept all with an evenness and tranquillity of spirit." This is, evidently, the counsel that should be followed, but, when the people who criticize a work are men of piety and worth, the saints themselves are troubled and disquieted. They begin to wonder whether they are following their own sweet will rather than the promptings of the Holy Spirit, and inspired by sense-illusions or diabolical suggestion.

It is a mistake to take quite simply for granted long after their death, that the saints were encouraged and inspired by the success and the definite triumph which they foresaw. The majority of them, when dying, could have made their own those words of Christ: " My God, my God, why have you abandoned me? " The qualities which are essential to the saints, as charity, humility, sweetness, austerity, independence, courage, perseverance, are all greatly admired by posterity; but they did not make the saints popular in their own lifetime. A close study of their lives will show that they were not nearly so esteemed by their contemporaries and brethren as is generally supposed. Indeed, they were little known. St. Francis of Assisi, at the moment of his death, saw himself vigorously opposed by the greater and more important part of his brethren, at the head of them being the highly influential Elias of Cortona.[1] Pope Gregory IX reproached severely the first sons of St. Dominic with neglecting the glory of their father. St. Alphonsus Liguori was, so to speak, cashiered by the Society he had founded. The discalced Carmelites, who had been reformed by St. John of the Cross, regarded the intelligence of the saint as sub-normal,

[1] See Cuthbert: *Life*, p. 383 and *passim*.

and Fra Elias de Misericordia declared that, had the Mystical Doctor lived longer, they would have deprived him of the religious Habit as they did to P. Gratien. St. Teresa of Avila, shortly before her death, met with an icy reception in the Carmel of Valladolid from her niece, who was also one of her earliest companions. A similar frigidity met her in the Carmel of Medina. She could not sleep, and in the grey of the morning, sick at heart, she went on her way. A short time later, she was dead.

It may be objected that contemplative souls suffer less from these contradictions, defections, and trials. It is evident that the monk, who gives himself as fully as possible to the life of solitude, escapes this kind of trial; but he is subject to others, to which, however, apostolic souls are no strangers either. We have said that the saints who are men of action, sometimes lose confidence in themselves by reason of the difficulties and the reverses with which they meet. For other reasons, or simply by divine permission, all the souls who seek after perfection, whether in the active life or—and especially—in the purely contemplative, ordinarily pass, sooner or later, through trying periods of scruples, of fears, and of anguish.

The most painful of all trials is undoubtedly that which a soul experiences, when, having renounced self and all things for the love of God, the soul comes to ask itself whether it really loves God, whether God really loves it, whether its whole life has not been, indeed, a tissue of illusions, of pride, and of hypocrisy. It is true, also, that a religious, who, like Soeur Thérèse of the Child Jesus, is haunted in her last years with doubts about the faith, suffers a trial no less exhausting. This, however, though specifically distinct, is very close to the preceding. All the great temptations against the love of God, against hope, against faith, against the love of the neighbour, if they are not of the same species, are of the same order. It can be said that it is impossible to arrive at holiness without passing through one or other of them. All souls called by God to a high perfection and who respond generously to that call, ought to strive to live that celebrated saying of St. Paul: *Foris pugnae, intus timores.* (II Cor. VII, 5.)

At this stage, an objection may be raised that, by treating successively the principal purifications through which holy souls pass, we have ignored a most delicate problem. It constantly happens that the soul who sets off to reach perfection, experiences very early consolation and light, but is very soon deprived of all such sensible and spiritual fervour, and must move in a desert place, pathless and without water. This is the trial usually sent to those who enter on the mystical life, properly so called. It is well to warn these souls, at the very beginning of this aridity, that there is no need for discouragement or self-blame.

We answer that it was not our intention to treat formally of the different passive purifications. They are, however, comprised in the trials we have listed as natural to the beginners. We emphasize, also, that the greatest mystics and the greatest saints, the Doctors, the Fathers, did not use the term " passive purification." We may hope, therefore, to attain to holiness, not indeed by escaping those hard providential trials which crucify flesh and spirit, but while neglecting to make a special study of the theories, recently and very usefully propounded by theologians, of passive purification. Directors of souls should, of course, know them, but such knowledge is superfluous for a soul that is neither sufficiently cultivated nor sufficiently prepared. It is sufficient that souls who sincerely desire to attain to perfection should humbly submit themselves to competent spiritual direction, and should be generous and patient in enduring the physical and moral sufferings which God sends them.

Care must be taken, however, not to confuse a trial relating to individual passive purification, with redemptory sufferings permitted for the salvation of the collectivity. It sometimes happens, indeed, that a fervent soul, who is vowed as a victim to merciful love or whom Our Lord wills to associate in a special manner with His Passion, passes through long and cruel sufferings to expiate the sins of its brethren in the faith or of the Lord's ministers. To interpret these sufferings by the theory of individual passive purification, when they really stem from the doctrine of the Communion of Saints and of vicarious satisfaction, would be an error which could have most regrettable consequences. Shortly before her death, Soeur Thérèse declared: " The chalice is filled to the brim; I cannot understand why I suffer so, except it be my extreme desire to save souls."

Finally, let us recognize that prudence, good sense aided by experience, by prayer, by the light of the Holy Spirit, can, in many cases, advantageously supply for special knowledge acquired from learned theological works. We must not forget that certain great trials are willed or permitted by Our Saviour in order that fervent souls may collaborate with His Passion and thus become co-redemptors. When a soul has reached this stage of perfection, the spiritual director is powerless to deliver it from these trials—scruples, doubts, temptations, despairing moods, etc.; but he can and should counsel perseverance in a meritorious struggle and confidence in the Divine mercy, always mindful of the Gospel words: " Peace to men of good will."

CHAPTER EIGHT

THE LOVE OF GOD

A<small>N</small> ardent love of God supposes the renunciation of sensible pleasures and the mortification of self-love, of the least movements of conupiscence and of all egoism; but it is also the cause of detachment from creatures and of self-abnegation. We would be indeed unhappy, said St. Teresa of Avila, if we could love God only when we had destroyed completely within ourselves sensible or too natural appetites. In practice, we begin loving God while we undertake the task of self-reformation. It is, then, by constantly mortifying ourselves and by giving ourselves to prayer that we arrive at the perfection of divine love.

The greatest happiness of man, even in this life, consists in the habitual practice of this love—a truth which the noblest of the pagan philosophers have proclaimed. Plato wrote: " O my dear Socrates, it is the vision of eternal beauty that can give a value to this our life. By comparison with that vision, of what worth are the riches and the friends you so esteem? . . . How great is the destiny of man to whom it shall be given to contemplate beauty without alloy, who shall see face to face the unique form of beauty." What Plato guessed at as an ideal of perfection and beatitude towards which man ought always to tend, the best among Christians have realized; but they would not have been able to attain to the summit of divine love, if a way and steps in a way had not been shown to them, and if they had not been assisted in their ascent by many helps and graces. It is important, certainly, that the end to be attained should be shown, but if it is made to appear, in practice, as an unapproachable ideal, no good purpose is served. To affirm that all our good consists in attaching ourselves to contemplation and to the Divine Beauty seems to imply, in effect, that we should live as angels. Now, in spite of the idealists, we affirm very plausibly that we are weighed down by matter, and therefore we cannot continue for long in sublime contemplation.

Christianity brings us something quite other than a cold and inaccessible ideal, by affirming that perfection consists, above all, in the love of God. Christ has revealed belief and love to us in a God Who loves us and Who has a father's concern for our good; He has told us that He Himself is God, only Son of the Father and equal to Him. He has lived among us, and before ascending into Heaven, He promised that He would not leave us, but that He would send His Holy Spirit to teach us all things.

When Plato shows us the divinity as " an eternal beauty," uncreated and imperishable, not subject to growth and diminution, nor to ugliness in one part balancing beauty in another, beautiful from one viewpoint and ugly from another—he really teaches us nothing about the divine life: when Christ speaks of God as the Father, the Son, and the Holy Ghost, and lays down the foundations on which the Fathers and the theologians have built the profound and ever mysterious doctrine of the Holy Trinity, He reveals to us the transcendent life of knowledge and of love which is the life of God. The saints who have reached the summit of perfection and who have attained to a life of union with the Holy Trinity have been plunged in this mystery as in an abyss of life and love, and have tasted of eternal life even on earth.

This perfect life is not ordinarily reached on earth, except after a long initiation. Spiritual authors never tire of repeating that the way we must take to arrive at this end is the humanity of Jesus Christ. St. Thomas says profoundly: " God became man in order that man should not love his fellow-man more than he loves God." The Word made flesh understood infinitely better than the greatest human minds, that the human heart has need of sensible love. That is why, in becoming incarnate, He willed to be one of us, to live humbly and to have, like us, a life-story. During His whole life and especially in His ministry, He showed His love for us in a palpable way. Men saw, heard and—so to speak—touched His loving mercy. Before Christ, no one had spoken of the goodness of God, or given to the world a living impression of that goodness as He did, when He told the parable of the Prodigal Son, or greeted tenderly, to the horror of the Pharisees, Magdalen the sinner. We recall here, because of the capital place which these mysterious facts hold in the life of the mystics, the lessons and proofs of humility and love which Jesus gave us, when He washed the feet of His disciples and when, a little later, He instituted the Sacrament in which He gave His Flesh to eat and His Blood to drink.

St. Teresa of Avila would seem to have been the best exponent, both in her life and her teaching, of how the humanity of Jesus is the way to the highest contemplation. The parts of her autobiography in which she develops the necessity of this devotion to the humanity of Christ, are classic and well known. We shall cite a few extracts.

Certain directors, in her day, were advocates of an exclusively spiritual contemplation, at least for those souls who had passed through the purgative and entered on the illuminative way. " They strongly recommend us," she writes, " to banish every corporal image, and to raise ourselves to the contemplation of the divinity; they consider the humanity itself of Jesus as a hindrance to contemplation; what should be attempted, according to them, is to consider . . . the humanity as penetrated with the Godhead. . . ." Whether they realized it or not, these doctors of spirituality were counselling the practice of a union with the Divinity or a mystical contemplation which resembled Neo-Platonism; but St. Teresa of Avila was both too experienced in the spiritual life and too little accustomed to speculations and abstractions to be for long led astray by this sublime and deceptive doctrine. Having followed for some time the teaching of these mystics, she was quick to notice the weakness it contained and the false conclusions to which it led. A woman of action more than of speculation, St. Teresa instinctively practised the experimental method: " When my prayer became a little supernatural, I attempted to remove all corporal images from my mind. I began, indeed, to experience the presence of God and I strove to keep myself recollected in Him. As this is a most agreeable prayer, no one could have made me return to the holy humanity of the Saviour." Thus, she found nothing but advantage in the counsels of her directors, but very soon she began to experience difficulties. " My soul," she says, " was in a terrible state, for it received consolation at intervals only, and apart from such times it was completely helpless in suffering and temptations." It is at this point that the saint discerns the erroneous principle underlying this excessively spiritualist thesis: " We are not angels," she says, " for we have a body. To attempt to play the angel on this earth is foolish. Ordinarily, we need a leaning-staff to our thought. When occupations, persecutions, pain trouble our repose; when dryness comes on us, Jesus Christ is our very good friend. He becomes a companion to us, and when we have accustomed ourselves to the thought, it is very easy to find Him standing close beside us."

It would seem that it requires only a little elementary good sense to recognize what is mistaken in such an idealistic and even quietist doctrine; but in every epoch fervent souls deceive themselves all too easily with these specious theories, which flatter their taste for the mystical states and promise an easy access to perfection. " We are not angels," says St. Teresa, " so let us not pretend to *walk in the air*." The saint uses language which recalls, by association, a celebrated saying of Pascal. Our love for God, even when it is very spiritual, is almost necessarily accompanied, in most cases, by sensible love, and this should have for its object the humanity of Christ. With reason does St. Teresa call the example of the saints to witness her opinion. St. Bernard, St. Francis, the first stigmatist, lived with Jesus as with an intimate friend, Whom they ceaselessly adored and with Whom they lived in respectful and sweet familiarity.

It has been justly remarked that the devotion to the Sacred Heart, as defined and divulged through St. Margaret Mary, had been as a new revelation of the tender love of Jesus Christ for men, which love in its turn calls for the love of men. Man, naturally distracted and indifferent to divine things, has need of being constantly, in every way, even in his sensibility, provoked by divine love.

Even the humanity of Christ has need of intermediaries. They presume on our good temper, who criticize the many forms of Christian devotion, and pretend to find in them the relics of polytheism and idolatry. The Curé d'Ars, so austere and so diffident of the human nature which he knew, through the Confessional, better than any man, was profoundly attached with a most tender affection to St. Philomena. It is not the least characteristic fact of the life of this ascetic, whose religious education was shadowed by Jansenism and whose austerities exceeded those of the desert fathers, that he felt an imperious need to confide in a young saint of fourteen years. " Between her and the holy priest," says Trochu, " there grew a chaste and mysterious love; she was his Beatrice, his ideal, his sweet star, his consolation, his pure light."

We have not sidetracked ourselves, because, as St. Thomas teaches, the love of the Blessed Virgin and the saints, and the love of the neighbour, are one with divine charity. (2ᵃ, 2ᵃᵉ, 25, art. 1.) A Christian has never truly loved God without having loved, at the same time, the saints and his fellow-men. Inversely, it must be noted that even human friendship, in so far as it is honest, is one of the steps to a pure love of God. In accordance with the traditional doctrine of the Church, we affirm that man must raise himself progressively, by continuous and unconscious steps, from the love of the creature to the love of God.

" Love," says St. Bernard, " finishes in the spirit but begins in the flesh ": a sentence which was not lightly thrown off, but given as the résumé of a whole doctrine of charity. Every time he treated of this doctrine of divine love, whether in his sermons on the *Canticle of Canticles* or in his treatise *De diligendo Deo*, he explains how the soul must raise itself from sensible creature to the Holy Trinity, by means of the Blessed Virgin and Christ. When for the first time we put our foot on the ladder of love, we are, by reason of the corruption of our nature and our acquired evil habits, much nearer to the animal than we are to the angel. That is why a legitimate love, even human, and, in general, a love for nature and for all that is beautiful, serve as a beginner of our ascent to God.

Theologians or spiritual authors who have not sufficient experience in spiritual direction or in Confessional work, have adopted a very strict attitude in this matter. Certainly, there comes a time in the soul's advance to perfection when it is useful, if not indeed necessary, to suppress all affection which could attract it to creatures and distract it from God; but, for the beginners, all honest love of the good and the beautiful is already progress, and even with the advanced, such love, when regulated, aids them to union with God. St. John of the Cross was very alive to this in his spiritual teaching. He writes: "There are souls who are very strongly attracted to God by means of sense objects, and this is excellent when the objects are not a hindrance and when their joy in them is lifted up to God. It is not necessary, therefore, to avoid such sense impressions, which can be the source of pious exaltation, but one can and should use them for the holy exercise of prayer and of the love of God."

What is said of beautiful and good things in general is said with much greater reason of legitimate friendship. St. Teresa of Avila, who had such a profound knowledge of the human heart and of the things about which she wrote, said: "If we behave with *moderation and discretion* in the affections which are not entirely spiritual, everything will become meritorious, and what apparently proceeds only from nature will result in virtue. Remembering our weakness, an affection of this kind—for example, for a saintly and wise spiritual guide—will help us greatly to realize mighty things for the service of God." Ordinarily, the picture of spiritual friendship painted for us is uncompromisingly perfect. "Let us begin," counsels St.

Teresa, " with practising it in a moderate degree, and even if a little tenderness mixes through it, no harm is done, provided there is nothing exclusive about the friendship. It can, of course, be said that such a friendship is not necessary, that God alone is sufficient for us, but for my own part, I assure you that I would now be in Hell but for friends of this kind."

We have said, and we maintain, that man, who is spirit and body, ought to use the sensible in order to rise to the spiritual, according to the teaching of St. John of the Cross. He should love God with his whole being, and therefore not only as a pure spirit loves, but also with sentiment, with tenderness. Once again, it is because He knew this sensible need of human love that the Word was made flesh, and it is for the same reason that Jesus showed Himself under the most touching of human conditions—in the manger, tired at the well, or allowing the beloved disciple to rest his head on His Heart at the last supper.

When due regard has been had to the sensitive part of our nature, it remains true that the soul, though strictly dependent on the senses, can become capable by habit, by sacrifice, by prayer, and above all by grace, of rising to a love of God which is spiritual and completely detached by the sensible appetite and even from all self-love. This is pure love, and it is needless to say that the number of souls who attain to the perfection of charity is relatively very small. In this matter of pure love, we must not create illusions which please and captivate us with their sublimity, but which is merely dangerous or deceptive. One often hears cited this important advice of St. John of the Cross: " When a soul has attained to a certain degree of this solitary love, it runs great risk both to itself and to the Church, if it wills, even for a few moments, to undertake exterior works, whatever their importance . . . because a little of such love is so precious before God, so useful to the soul and of such value to the Church, that its apparent inaction is richer than the sum of all good works." This is certainly true; but souls who have begun to taste supernatural prayer, the prayer of recollection or the prayer of quiet, should not persuade themselves that this advice is for them.

Indeed, St. John of the Cross here addresses himself to souls who have attained to the state of union. Now, if souls called to a true contemplative life are not few, those among them who are raised to the spiritual marriage or to the habitual practice of pure love, are rare exceptions. St. Bernard, already arrived at a high degree of holiness, wrote: " I do not know if, in this life, anyone has ever attained that high degree of love in which man does not love himself more than he loves God. . . . We are told that such love has been experienced; for my part, I must admit, this seems impossible." St. Francis de Sales, who loved to repeat that well-known saying: " Self-love dies a quarter of an hour after us," thought that the perfect love of God could be met with very seldom on this earth. St. Thomas Aquinas held the same view, and would seem to have settled the question with precision, when, treating of the virtues commanded by perfect charity, he wrote: " They are the virtues of those who have acquired a divine resemblance, and they are therefore called the virtues of the completely purified soul: in such sort, that prudence is concerned only with divine matters; that temperance has no longer to combat the sense appetites; that fortitude no longer knows the pull of passion; that justice, in fine, conforms to the divine thought by a perpetual union—and such virtues, we think, are those of the Blessed or of very perfect souls on earth."

A perfection so rare and so exempt from strife would seem to be unnecessary in the state of pure love. Does not history show us that it is not necessarily required? For example, St. Thérèse of the Child Jesus experienced, in her last illness and shortly before her death, little motions of impatience. But, in such cases, it is because God allows this in order that merit may grow. A very holy soul can, it is true, be united to God by a most ardent and most pure love, and yet experience, as its contribution to the salvation of a greater number of men, temptations of certain passions of the spirit or of the senses. They are occasions of the greatest victories, but it is to be clearly understood that such temptations, however grave, are constantly repulsed and never penetrate into the sanctuary of the will where divine union is accomplished.

These preliminaries disposed of, we come to the essential condition of pure love. The question to be faced is whether a soul can reach complete self-abnegation, so as not to cede habitually to self-love, and thus to love God for Himself.

The sinner or the half-and-half Christian is converted to a more perfect love through a motive of the love of God, it is true, but also from personal interest: because he fears to die in sin, to lose Heaven or to suffer Hell. This partly interested love became insupportable to St. Thérèse, when she had entered Carmel and was already far advanced in the way of perfection. She said: " There is a verse in Psalm 118 which I can hardly bring myself to recite—that in which the just man says: I have inclined my heart to observe thy laws for ever because of the recompense." Without wishing to multiply the degrees of divine love, we can say that this is the first: To love God because He is supremely lovable, but also to obtain the reward and to avoid the punishment.

When a soul has preserved its Baptismal innocence, or, having sinned grievously, has years since returned to a state of grace, so as to have progressed in virtue and charity and the habit of serving God; when, for God's sake, it has mortified all its passions, devoted itself fervently to good works, and collaborated with the work of the Holy Spirit by prayer, by meditation, by corresponding with grace, by generous acceptance of suffering, by frequent union with the Eucharistic Christ—then, the fear of eternal punishment and the anxiety for recompense gradually lose their motive power. The soul arrives thus at the second degree of charity. The element of self-interest is not easily perceptible at this stage, but it can and generally does, in fact, enter in, unconsciously at least. However mortified the passions may be by ascetic exercises and by trials courageously borne, the roots remain, and sometimes these passions can suddenly make themselves felt again. Even in a work undertaken to please God, one can be surprised and humiliated to find an over-susceptibility, a nicety on a point of personal honour, pointing the fact that one's self-abnegation is not complete. More than that, according to a celebrated remark of St. Francis de Sales, one can have, even in the pursuit of virtue, an over-anxiety and too much love for one's own personal excellence. A very virtuous soul can, at times, desire perfection for perfection itself—that is to say, for the eminent superiority which it confers. The highest virtue can easily become a dangerous temptation to pride, so true it is that, in the most elevated states, the soul must be extremely careful of what Pascal calls: *libido excellendi*, the passion to excel.

The third and last degree of charity supposes, then, that the soul must love God for His own sake, with an habitual, perfectly complete abnegation of self. Before attaining to this ultimate perfection, the saints have desired, ordinarily, with great desire, the cruellest sufferings and even martyrdom and annihilation. " I have never doubted," wrote M. Olier to Marie Rousseau, " that the heart of Christianity is in suffering." In the same sense, he wrote to his director: " To love in suffering is, I believe, the true mark of love." That suffering is essential to Christianity, for the ransom of our sins and the salvation of our souls, we have shown to be incontestable. St. John of the Cross has shown splendidly the need for suffering. Before reaching the stage of perfect love, souls have lived for the greater part of their time with a consciousness of their own unworthiness, such " that they have seen Hell opened to swallow them for eternity. It can be literally said that they descended alive into Hell. . . . Again, they have been so engulfed by profound sorrow that their interior torment has overflowed in tears and groaning." Such tortures are unspeakable, yet those who aspire to high holiness can expect no less.

Convinced that they purify themselves more and more, and at the same time contribute to the salvation of souls, by these sufferings, the saints have desired ardently to meet with opprobrium and scorn, because they have recognized that these are necessary to destroy in themselves the least germs and roots of self-love and pride. Our Lord appeared to St. John of the Cross and asked him what he desired. The saint replied: " *Contemni et pati pro te*—To be contemned and to suffer for Thee." This ardent thirst for scorn became, with the great saints, a kind of real joy. . . . This paradoxical joy can appear disconcerting to us, but reflection will show that the source of this joy for the saints is the ever-growing knowledge that they are becoming daily more and more identified with Christ crucified.

It can, however, be asked whether these extremely ardent desires for suffering and humiliation are the highest point of divine love. Having passed through the stage of sorrows and scorn, it would seem that many saints experience an appeasement before their death, because they come to desire nothing in particular, save only to unite their will with that of Our Lord. They have acquired the habit of conforming their wills always and unhesitatingly to the Will of Christ, so that the union of their souls with the Soul of Christ has become a kind of identification, and, as it were, a unity rather than a union. *Vivo autem, jam non ego; vivit vero in me Christus.* (Gal. xi, 20.)

This truth, which may seem mysterious or contestable, becomes more acceptable to our minds if we consider the lives and example of the saints. Soeur Thérèse of the Child Jesus ardently desired sufferings and humiliations during the greater part of her religious life. When she pronounced her vows, she carried next her heart a prayer for the martyrdom of spirit and body. In the last year of her life, she experienced a great appeasement, and her soul was no longer a prey to great desires, even to that of suffering. Mère Agnes de Jésus testifies: " She expresses in her biography the extreme desire which she had for martyrdom; but, towards the end, when she had reached the summit of perfection, she experienced an appeasement which made her say: I no longer desire either suffering or death, though I cherish them both. I have known suffering, and I have thought to touch the shores of Heaven; to-day, self-abandonment is my only guide and I have no other compass. I can no longer ask anything with ardour, except the perfect accomplishment of the Will of God in my soul. . . . Her conformity to the Will of God exceeded even her desire for martyrdom and for heaven."

This absolute conformity to the Divine Will is what characterizes the highest degree of the love of God. St. Francis de Sales wrote to St. Chantal: " This morning, I was absolutely unable to ponder on an eternity of Heaven which awaits us . . . except in so far as it took the form of an unvarying and ever actual love of the great God Who reigns eternally, so that, if Hell was a fire of God's love, its torments would seem desirable to me." Statements of this kind are met with from saints who have reached this state of perfection. They know perfectly well that such statements could have no real relation to reality, but, feeling the need to show to what extent their will is conformed to the Will of God, and in order to assuage the love that devours them they go the length of saying that Hell would be Heaven to them, if in it they could accomplish the Divine Will. In this context, St. Francis de Sales writes: " While resignation is practised through effort and submission, very holy indifference, which is far above resignation, loves nothing except through love of the Divine Will. It matters nothing whether the Will of God is expressed in me through suffering or consolation; whether, when I am sick, I get well or die, provided I do not desire or seek anything except the Divine Will."

This love of God's Will for that Will itself, is therefore the summit of perfection; it is the culminating point to which we must tend without easily persuading ourselves that we have attained it. We could, indeed, grievously deceive ourselves and nothing could be more deplorable than to live in an easy mediocrity, thinking we are at a high summit of virtue, while in reality we are stagnating in a lukewarm spiritual morass. We, who are not saints, ought to be extremely distrustful of self, and, while avoiding scrupulosity, we ought to examine ourselves sincerely in the recollection of prayer. One day, at the time when her Vows had been postponed for eight months, meditating on Père Surin's *Foundations of the Spiritual Life*, St. Thérèse made this comment: " I understood in prayer that a great deal of self-love was mixed with my very ardent desire to pronounce my Vows." How many, in similar circumstances, having neither the humility nor the clearsightedness of the holy Carmelite, would have been unaware that this self-love which insinuates itself into a supernatural desire, could have nothing to do with Our Lord. Yet it is frequently met with, as the dross in a truly real love of God, in an ardent zeal which inspires the holiest desires and gives strength to support crosses for God's glory and to undertake many and meritorious works. How many imperfections mix with these desires at their birth, or cloud them in their execution? Without, then, supernatural proofs sanctioned by a spiritual director, it would be an unpardonable presumption to believe oneself to be raised to the highest mansion, where one tastes pure love. On the other hand, to be discouraged by the difficulty of arriving at such perfection would be a certain sign that pride is still alive in us. Souls who put themselves to the school of spiritual infancy, so warmly recommended by St. Thérèse, ought to follow her example by humiliating themselves and resigning themselves to being always imperfect, without, however, neglecting to examine themselves for the smallest imperfections, and by the grace of God correcting them. Let us practise the counsel which St. John gives us in the Apocalypse: " He that is just, let him become yet more just; and he that is holy, let him become holier still."

Chapter Nine

THE LOVE OF THE NEIGHBOUR

" I AM going to write about fraternal charity," said
Soeur Thérèse to Mère Agnes de Jésus, " because I
feel bound to do so, seeing how little charity is understood
on earth." The young saint referred to a truth very much
more unknown than is generally thought.

We state a paradox that will astonish many readers: it
is every bit as difficult to love one's neighbour perfectly
as it is to love God. This statement is based on the truth
that, according to the Thomistic doctrine, the virtue or
habitus of the love of God is not specifically different from
the virtue of *habitus* of the love of the neighbour, and
therefore, perfection in the one is as difficult to acquire
as perfection in the other.

Notice well that for the moment we are not concerned
with the love of the neighbour under what is commonly
regarded as its most difficult aspect—the love of one's
enemies. We believe that if one strives after perfection in
the love of one's nearest and dearest, one undertakes a
more difficult task than that involved in the general love
of benevolence we must give to our enemies, and moreover, that it is impossible of attainment without the aid
of divine grace. We will take a familiar example which
will throw great light on the subject and will anticipate
many objections. Ordinarily, mothers passionately love

their children and would give their lives for them; yet, how few are the Christian mothers who love their children perfectly. Is there any need to insist on this? All around us, we have examples of mothers who spare no pains in bringing up their sons, who deprive themselves of necessities to secure for them a brilliant future, yet whose devotion is coloured by much egoism, by vanity, by ambition or by other regrettable faults which vitiate and make harmful this maternal love.

What is said of maternal love can, with even greater reason, be applied to the love which friends bear to each other in the world. We speak here of very warm friendships. At first, they seem very praiseworthy, but when one has had time to study intimately the nature of the affection friends bear each other, how many deplorable defects are discovered. Jealousy is often found, and, at least with one of the parties, egoism and that tendency to dominate which deprives the other of the independence and liberty without which the higher faculties of one's personality cannot be brought into play. In such cases, love ceases to be love, in the highest sense of the word, and becomes, according to the expression of St. Thomas, a love of concupiscence. An immediate conclusion from all this is that it is advantageous, from one view-point, to be so loved, and from another, burdensome. How frequently, alas, have the children of even Christian parents, realizing a call to exercise great talents towards an exceptional destiny, been obliged to fight with firmness and perseverance the shortsightedness and prejudices of their parents. What tremendous vocations, artistic, literary, military, have been realized only after painful tearing of souls.

In the case of religious vocations, properly so-called, the most tender affection of relations, of close friends, even when they are Christian, shows itself in an astonishingly narrow and egoistic fashion. St. Francis of Assisi stripped himself as an expression of his opposition to his father's efforts to thwart his vocation. St. Thomas Aquinas would not have become the great theologian whose doctrine we followed, had he not first obeyed the call of God, against the loud and organized ambition of his family.

There is nothing better, from one point of view, than to be passionately loved by someone: yet, it is also true that there is scarcely anything which can so make us fail in our destiny and paralyse us. The Biblical example given us is that of Samson and Delila. In the beginning Delila was probably not the vulgar and disloyal courtesan which she later became, and Samson was not the simple and naïve man we think him. Strengthened by the Holy Spirit, having received from on high the mission to save his people, he allowed the secret of his strength to be coaxed from him, little by little, because affection had made him soft. Samson's history can be told with other names in other ages and in every age, for as long as the world endures, the most eminent men, the most intelligent, and the most energetic in the accomplishment of a God-given task, will allow themselves to be surprised and overcome by a too-human love.

We must love our neighbour as ourselves, it has been said. This precept must be carefully interpreted. In the majority of cases, men love themselves so badly and with such a love of concupiscence, that, were they to love their neighbour as they love themselves, great damage would result. All around us are examples of the mean and the prodigal, of men whose only concern is to develop their inferior faculties, to enjoy the pleasures and goods of this world, of men who do not know how to govern themselves, and who are lacking in elementary prudence. Such can certainly not be asked to love their neighbours as themselves. There is a wise proverb: " Well-ordered charity begins at home "—i.e., with oneself. But, if the circumstances are examined in which this principle is invoked, one often finds that it is made the excuse for the worst egoism and for the taking of the lion's share.

It will, of course, be objected that it is Christ Himself Who commands us to love our neighbour as ourselves, and therefore, to make of our love of self the rule and measure for our love of the neighbour. The objection is easily answered.

Our Saviour undoubtedly said: " Thou shalt love thy neighbour as thyself." But He first affirmed, and the worldly are only too anxious to forget it: " This is the second command, and it is like unto the first: Thou shalt love the Lord thy God with thy whole heart, and with thy soul, and with all thy mind and with all thy strength. This is the greatest and the first commandment." To separate the second commandment from the first and to consider it in isolation, is to fall into a grave error: it is, if we may use a comparison, to remove the first storey of a building and expect the second to stand on air. Love of self cannot be made the criterion or rule of the love of our neighbour, if we do not first love God with all our powers. Otherwise, our self-love is a heathen thing, defective, too human, too egoistic, and it would then be extremely dangerous to love the neighbour as oneself.

It is, however, exact to say that, if a person subordinates himself in all things to the will of God, he ought to seek, before all else and for the love of God, his own eternal salvation. Even if the hypothesis were feasible, one ought not to commit the least sin for the salvation of humanity, because to commit a sin would be to begin to oppose the

Divine Will. It can, therefore, be justly said that well-ordered charity begins with oneself: but it must be understood, as it could be better expressed: well-ordered charity begins with God. If we love ourselves absolutely as God wills, then we can love our neighbour absolutely as we love ourselves; but, if in the order of charity, we remove the love of God, which is the foundation of the whole structure, every other secondary principle and all deductions are lacking in foundation, and therefore collapse.

We now ask how God wills that we should love the neighbour. Those who tend to perfection ought to love their neighbours with a truly spiritual or wholly super-natural love. To love one's neighbours with a truly spiritual love is to wish, not only their salvation, but as much as possible their perfection on earth. Soeur Thérèse of the Infant Jesus founded her doctrine of fraternal charity on that word of Christ: " A new commandment I give unto you, that you love one aother as I have loved you." And she has explained, in a very clear manner, this doctrine of absolutely disinterested love, which has sometimes been subtly interpreted by the greatest Doctors of the Church. On the principle of her conduct, she writes: " When I understood that of myself I could do nothing, the task seemed simplified for me. I would occupy myself entirely and interiorly uniting myself more and more to God, knowing that the rest would be given to me in the overflow." To unite oneself to God, in the language of St. Thérèse who asked Christ to remain in her always as at the moment of Communion, means first of all to unite oneself to Christ. It means, she says, to be no longer two—to disappear in the love of the Divine Master as a drop of water loses itself in the ocean— to act, not by one's own will, but by divine strength.

Remembering that the Divine Master lived in her, she could declare: " I feel, when I am charitable, that it is Jesus alone Who acts in me; the more I am His, the more I love the Sisters." Careful to penetrate and to observe in all its detail the precept of charity, Soeur Thérèse set herself to study carefully how the Divine Master had loved His Disciples. She remarked that it was not precisely for their natural qualities, since, she justly says, " they were ignorant and filled with earthly thoughts." A study of the Gospel shows with what patience Christ supported the very human and Jewish imperfections of His Apostles and Disciples. Sometimes, indeed, they seemed to irritate Him. " O unfaithful and perverse generation," He cries, " how long shall I be with you, how long shall I suffer you? " We shall explain, later, how this holy anger, deliberate and willed, was inspired by the divine love which He bore to His disciples. But Jesus was ordinarily sweet and patient with them, for He knew that the men whom He addressed could not understand Him, even though they loved Him. He relied on time and on the assistance of the Holy Spirit, Whom He would send after His death on his Church, as yet in the throes of its birth.

It must be especially remembered that, certain reserves being made, true love of the neighbour is principally concerned with being patient in our relations with him. One of the principal characteristics of charity, according to St. Paul, is that of benevolent patience: *Caritas patiens est benigna est.* Except in particular cases, we are not officially charged with the care of the neighbour, with expressly directing him in holiness, but we ought always to help him, and show our benevolence towards him as much as we can. Soeur Thérèse, who in the last years of her life could find food for prayer in the Gospel only, makes this instructive and very important remark: " In meditating on the divine words, I have seen how imperfect was my love for my Sisters, because I did not love them as Jesus loves them. Now I know that true charity consists in supporting all the faults of the neighbour, in not being surprised at his weaknesses, and in being edified by his least virtues."

It can therefore be maintained that the primordial attribute of charity, as of Christian strength, is the bearing with the imperfections of the neighbour. Souls who have advanced somewhat in the spiritual life and who enter into a state of union with God, ought not to forget this attribute of divine love. They have sharp eyes through long years of self-examination and self-correction, and therefore they easily discern in their most devout friends or in the community to which they belong, imperfections and faults, often very real and regrettable indeed, which prevent progress in holiness and paralyse the efficacy of the apostolate. A soul that has gone to school to the saints, and has caught their love of poverty, of chastity, of obedience, of mortification, of silence, of regularity, is very liable to suffer from the failure in the observation of vows, of virtues, of evangelical counsels, which it sees often occurring around it. A lukewarm Christian does not even notice these failures, which have acquired the ease of habit, and so far from being hurt by them, he often finds them a source of content.

If, however, a fervent soul notices certain relaxations of discipline gaining ground in its circle, and habitually experiences irritation and trouble in consequence, such a soul is very far from the state of union. Indeed, in spite of an opinion to the contrary too often admitted, those who, though virtuous and truly spiritual, are inspired by a bitter zeal to wish to reform those about them, to ruthlessly correct their friends, are still only beginners, very far from the goal of perfection. In the first years of her religious life, Soeur Thérèse had passed through the stage of being over-solicitous for the amendment of the neighbour; but, later on when she was officially charged with the direction of the novices, she corrected this somewhat immoderate care and thought only of how best she could accept and excuse the imperfections of the neighbour. As Mistress of Novices, she rejoiced that she was not obliged to correct any Sister whom she saw breaking a rule, and she " proceeded forthwith to seek diligently to excuse the offender by attributing good intentions to her."

Apart from those who are invested with a special charge of souls, it can be maintained that a soul who is engaged in acquiring perfection ought, for that very reason, to labour more to bear patiently the faults of the neighbour than to correct them. Zeal, even when apparently most legitimate, is easily twisted by suggestions which come from nature. In this context, St. John of the Cross says: " The elevation of a soul, established in a definitive manner in the state of union, is so great that, though formerly it was tossed by the waters of sorrow and afflicted by the bitterness which the sins of others can cause, now it no longer experiences this, even while it appreciates more perfectly than ever the destruction wrought by sin. . . . Such a soul is in a state which resembles that of the angels who understand perfectly the effects of evil without knowing its sorrow, who perform their works of mercy without experiencing the sorrow of compassion."

We conclude, then, with the Scripture, that the measure of a man's holiness will be, above all, the measure of his patience and benevolence. " Learn of me," said Christ, " because I am meek and humble of heart."

When we have thus established the primordial necessity

of patience, we must hasten to add that the saints, when their duty involved fraternal correction, did not shirk their obligations.

St. Paul, who constantly emphasized charity and the sweetness of charity—*non irritatur, omnia suffert, omnia sustinet*—has used, when he felt it his duty, words and acts of such violence that they would undoubtedly scandalize many Christians to-day. There was the famous scene in which he faced St. Peter: " I resisted Peter to his face," he writes, " because he was reprehensible." We once knew a very saintly and learned Religious, exercising a very high charge, who could not understand very well this manner of acting on the part of the great Apostle. The attitude of Peter, he said, tempering with wisdom the observation made to him, is most worthy of admiration. However, when the history of the young Church is more carefully examined, and one remembers the strength of Jewish prejudices and the great importance of the universal or catholic mission of St. Paul; when the precise circumstances of the development of Christianity in Antioch are appreciated, where the great question at issue was whether the nations were to become Christian through accepting the Mosaic Law or whether they were to be freed from its yoke—then it becomes easy to understand that St. Paul, divinely and very specially appointed by Christ as the promoter of universal Christianity, should have used all his power and vehemence, at this critical moment, in favour of the cause to which he had devoted his life. A very vehement intervention, in certain exceptional cases, is absolutely necessary.

The biographies of the saints are rich in examples. St. Bernard, in his *Apologia* of the Cistercians in favour of religious reform, thought it his absolute duty to denounce vigorously and in detail, the relaxations of the Cluniacs.

Peace-loving Christians of to-day scarcely appreciate such language, and a work like that of the Founder of Clairvaux would very probably not be supported. It will be objected, of course, that there is question, in the historical case we quote, of an exceptional saint whose virtue, eloquence, and miracles had acquired an extraordinary prestige. We answer that St. Bernard is not considered here with the aura of eight centuries' fame around his actions, for, when he wrote his burning *Apologia*, he was simply Br. Bernard, twenty-eight years old, who had neither preached in public nor worked any wonder. The greater part of the Christian world understood, nevertheless, that the frequently passionate zeal of the very young Abbot of Clairvaux had its justification, that it was inspired by supernatural zeal and by the purest charity.

We have implied that the Christian outlook of our day has softened and even become insipid. The impetuous excesses of the saints are no longer understood or admitted, because they seem exaggerated. " That we may recognize in violence an enemy to be combated," says a modern hagiographer, " it suffices to consider, firstly, that it is not in order, since it deprives the soul, if only for an instant, of its equilibrium and its self-possession, and that it verges, through impatience which is a fault, on anger, which is a vice and a source of sins; again, its effect is injurious to souls, since it cows them when it should entice them; finally, and above all perhaps, it is contrary to the Gospel which proclaims the beatitude of the meek."

This eulogy of a meekness which absolutely excludes all kind of anger, undoubtedly contains a great deal of truth. Nevertheless, it is disconcerting at first to compare it with the doctrine of St. Thomas. In the *Summa* (2^a 2^{ae}, 9. 158, art. 1), he poses the question whether it is ever lawful to allow oneself to grow angry, and he answers without hesitation: "He who gives place to anger without reason is culpable, but he who does so with reason is entirely innocent; because, if anger were never shown, there would be no progress in doctrine, rules would not be observed, faults would not be reproved." St. Thomas, who had himself given such noble example of patience and courage, concluded: "If anyone is angry in a just measure, then his action is lawful. *Tunc irasci est laudabile.*" And, as if he foresaw the objections which his doctrine would not fail to meet with from the spirituals of his own and of every age, he insists that anger which is a consequence of reasoned reflection is praiseworthy, and is rightly called holy anger: *Haec ira est bona, quae dicitur ira per zelum.* In this context, he cites the authority of St. Gregory the Great, and he remarks that, if an anger inspired by holy zeal paralyses for a moment all deliberation of the reason, this is in no way contrary to the just conception of virtue, since it is quite normal that the reflection should cease when the moment of execution comes. It does not suffice, therefore, to condemn all impetuosity that one should say, as was said above: "It is not in order, since it deprives the soul, if only for an instant, of its equilibrium and its self-possession."

It would be useful for certain mystics, who, from a misunderstanding of the nature of love for the neighbour, recommend exclusively and without allowing the least attenuation, the exercise of patience and sweetness, to meditate on this question of the *Summa* which we have indicated. It would be to their very great advantage to study attentively the article in which St. Thomas asks: Is there a vice which arises from the lack of anger?— and answers in the affirmative. "He who is not angry when he has a good reason to be so, sins; because exaggerated patience sows vice, promotes negligence, and

invites to evil, not only the bad, but also the good."
St. Thomas concludes firmly: " The absence of anger in
such circumstances is, without doubt, a sin. *Absque dubio
est peccatum.*"

Many conscientious persons, willing to practise in its
perfection the love of the neighbour by the education of
the young, will recognize the necessity of acting sometimes
with vehement zeal.

St. Thérèse of the Child Jesus ordinarily behaved with
untiring patience. The promoter of her Cause, astonished
at hearing nothing but eulogy, asked her sister if she had
not remarked in her some small, habitual imperfection.
" She sometimes showed severity," was the anwer, " in
the formation of the novices, but I could not truly say
that this was a fault, for it was a holy anger." The saint
herself had written: " I would rather receive a thousand
reproaches than make one, but I feel that it is very
necessary that the need to make reproaches should be a
source of suffering to me."

The young saint, whom Providence intended as a
lesson and a model to our generation, practised sweetness
through charity, and was conciliatory as long as her
conscience permitted her; but, when the occasion arose,
that same charity for the neighbour inspired her to be
intrepid, and to fear nothing from inconvenience that
might result from her intrepidity. Through a special
permission, she was allowed to have spiritual conversation
with her sister, who was much older than Thérèse. The
saint noticed that her sister had a too sensible love of her
prayer, and, after long reflection, she spoke to her: " If
you continue to act as you are doing, you will cease to
obey your Rule and you will place your soul in great
danger. It is not true love of the neighbour which inspires you, but rather self-love; moreover, you may tell

the Mother Prioress what I have said, for I would rather be sent from the convent than fail to fulfil my whole duty." In an exceptional set of circumstances, when she was in some way charged with the spiritual direction of the Novices, she dared to say publicly before fifteen Sisters: " Mère Marie de Gouzague is absolutely wrong; it is an evident abuse of power to act as she has done; what pains me most is to see the good God offended in this matter." Certainly, if Soeur Thérèse had consulted merely human prudence, she would have held her peace and endeavoured to win the good grace of her who, a month or so after this outburst, was to be re-elected Prioress. The majority of those who listened to her were indignant, believing that she had acted through pure impulse; but, as the advocate of the saint remarked during the Process, she certainly acted under the inspiration of the Holy Spirit. " The Servant of God," he affirmed, " was worthy of all praise, when, moved by zeal for justice and for the Divine honour, she did not hesitate to expose herself to the anger of her who, in virtue of her prestige, might soon be elected Prioress, and could easily exact what reprisals she wished."

We have purposely insisted on the complete traditional and Thomistic doctrine which recommends, above all, patience towards the neighbour, but requires in certain circumstances, under pain of sin, that force—even vehement force—should be used, because this, when judiciously employed, also contributes very efficaciously to the sanctification of the neighbour and therefore to the greatest glory of God. The Angelic Doctor teaches that the principal characteristic of the virtue of fortitude is to know how to endure, but he immediately adds that the second characteristic is to know how to rouse oneself against an abuse or an evil with great intrepidity.

It may be asked if the mind of the Catholic people has been integrally formed, in this matter, by Christian educators. As Pius XI pointed out, the current conception of holiness is of something insipid. Is not this borne out by the characterless statues and images of our saints we see on all sides: have we not too exclusively taught, by our sermons, our books, our publications, that a man cannot be perfectly charitable, cannot be a saint, unless he is constantly sweet, patient, humble, resigned, always with the bit in his mouth ready to endure anything. A striking example of this partial and partly erroneous interpretation is found in the biography of the Curé d'Ars by the Abbé Monnin. Inspired, unconsciously, by his desire to edify the great majority of his Christian readers, he taught that the Curé d'Ars had always acted with sweetness in his sermons and catechetical instructions, "that he never reproached his parishioners. Mgr. Convert, who later became the Curé of the parish, very rightly remarked: "This is simply naïve. It would have been vain to expect the disorders of the parish to collapse of their own accord, as the walls of Jericho fell to the trumpets." All the evidence we possess flagrantly contradicts this interpretation of Monnin. Indeed, in the third volume of the works of M. Vianney, there is a sermon in which he explains to the faithful that there is a holy anger which comes from love for the neighbour and from zeal for the house of God.

It must be carefully noticed that there is often a very great difference between real love of the neighbour, and what the world calls amiability and politeness. How many cases could be cited, in which worldly courtesy is the very opposite of the supernatural love of the neighbour. "Those who possess true spiritual love," says Soeur Thérèse, " use no artifice towards the persons whom they love most. If there is the slightest deviation from the straight way, there are immediate warnings and censure. . . ." Charity to the neighbour, thus understood, supposes, therefore, a constant exercise of sweetness, but also of frankness and fortitude.

When these remarks have been made and admitted, we hasten to repeat, because it cannot be too often said, that the virtue of charity supposes, above all and always, the exercise of patience in every trial. It is for the very reason that a soul has long and sweetly borne with all the faults of the neighbour, and given every proof of evangelical sweetness, that, in certain circumstances, its ardent zeal will cause it to reflect on itself and its surroundings and to recognize, finally, the need for vigorous intervention. Sweetness and Christian fortitude have value only in so far as they complement each other, being each commanded and exercised by charity. By modifying it a little, we can apply to our context a famous *pensée* of Pascal: "I do not admire the excellence of a virtue, if I do not at the same time see the excellence of its contrary virtue: to act otherwise is not to mount, but to fall." It was by the practice, in an eminent degree, of the humble and manly virtues that the true disciples of Christ succeeded, following their Master, in reforming abuses and in contributing most efficaciously to the establishment of the Kingdom of God and to the salvation of men.

Chapter Ten

" MANY CALLED, FEW CHOSEN "

A QUESTION of great importance on which we have not even touched, must have occurred more than once to the reader's mind. We have treated of the general means which we ought to employ in order to attain sanctity: but are we *called* to sanctity? Is it not true that such a call is a special—even an extraordinary—grace, reserved to a very small number of souls?

We remark at the outset, as we have said expressly in the Preface, that this study is meant for fervent souls, for members of pious associations, and even for Religious. We have in view, therefore, an *élite*—an *élite* which, thank God, is relatively numerous in the Church. It is an incontestable fact of experience, however, that the number of pious souls or of Religious who attain to habitual union with God or to a superior state of the spiritual life, are very rare.

The Gospel phrase: *Multi vocati, pauci vero electi* is, at least with reference to sanctity, to be understood literally. We do not mean sanctity in the very general sense, possessed by all those in the state of grace, who are an effective part of the Communion of Saints and, in that sense, are saints. But we reserve the qualification of sanctity to the souls who possess eminent charity and eminent virtues. We must not join the foolishly optimistic, therefore, but we must realize that, as thus defined, sanctity is the prerogative of the very few. Much has been written lately on this subject. The two affirmations contained in the statement cited, must be absolutely attended to. It must not be concluded that, because there are few of the elect in the kingdom of holiness, that there are few of the called; nor must it be concluded from the fact that many are called to perfection and holiness, that, thanks to our efforts and industry, there could be many elect. There will always be, as Christ said, many called and few chosen.

This principle clearly understood, the question immediately arises: Why are many called and so few chosen? Many answers could be given. The first is that the majority of souls do not obtain from God sufficient grace to attain to holiness in our sense, that is, to complete detachment from all earthly things and intimate union with God. But a little reflection shows that this is simply to say, in other words, that few are chosen, while we must hold to the first part of the truth—that many are called. On the other hand, ascetical and mystical writers are unanimous in holding that God gives to all fervent souls and souls of good will, and especially to Religious, the grace which can contribute to their sanctification on earth. It would be superfluous to choose quotations from the Fathers and the Saints in support of this. The references to it are many and explicit.

" There are a great many souls," says St. Teresa of Avila, " who arrive at the first stage of supernatural recollection and quietude; but those who pass beyond this are few, and I know not who is here to blame. Very decidedly, God cannot be held responsible. On His side, having once accorded so great a favour, He does not cease to be prodigal towards us, at least in so far as our infidelity does not choke the stream of his graces."

If this great number of pious souls do not attain to perfection, the reason must be sought in certain infidelities to grace. One meets, however, with confessors and authors even—writing, it is true, as authors and not as theologians—who do not share this opinion. They hold that pious souls do not attain to the state of union for diverse and accidental reasons: lack of natural gifts of intelligence and will, need of proper direction, pull of an environment where certain poor ways of sanctity are followed, and so forth; loss of direction in a multitude of small devotions. To all this, they add that many people, even when fervent and well-intentioned, inherit or contract in their youth certain defects which it would require little short of a miracle to eradicate.

We do not deny that there is much truth in all this. Evidently, if a person is lacking in intelligence, it is extremely difficult to persuade him of his faults and failings. Nevertheless, it is also true that less gifted souls can, through the practice of obedience, rise to sanctity as quickly as those of the highest intelligence. But, while admitting that there are many hereditary and acquired mental and moral infirmities, which are as difficult to cure as physical infirmities, it must also be remembered that there are a great many souls who possess sufficient qualities to attain, with God's grace, to a high perfection.

It is an observation of St. Teresa's that often confessors are very broad and show *an excessive discretion*. " One of my confessors," she writes, " to whom I disclosed my scruples on the subject of my relations with persons of the world, told me one day that, when I would be elevated to sublime contemplation, these companions and these conversations would be no hindrance to me." The greatest attention must be paid, therefore, to sacrifices which can seem futile in themselves, but which are of capital importance when dealing with the spiritual progress of souls called to perfection.

In this connection, St. John of the Cross distinguishes venial sins and the smallest movements of appetite which constitute " simple imperfections," and he unhesitatingly maintains that the smallest of these, at least in so far as it is habitual and deliberate, ought to be completely eliminated, if one desires to attain to union. In this important matter, St. John is careful to go into details. As examples of habitual imperfections, he cites " talkativeness, small attachments to person, place or thing (a garment, a cell, a book), which one refuses to break off; each of these imperfections, if habitual, can retard the soul more than if one fell every day into many other imperfections, even more serious and venial, which did not arise from an acquired habit."

Perhaps those authors who too easily maintain that many souls fail, blamelessly, to attain to sanctity, have not sufficiently pondered these words of St. John. What can appear of little consequence in a mediocre soul, can often be of very great importance in a soul called by God to a high perfection.

It may be objected that an experienced and competent confessor or director is very difficult and often impossible to find. It is a very grave and delicate matter to confide one's soul to a confessor, who will be at the same time director of one's conscience and whom one must obey even in the least details. St. Teresa of Avila often said that she had a long search for an experienced and enlightened director. She was at first under the guidance of a priest who was, she says, of noble birth and high intelligence, but who had no knowledge of the ways of spirituality. He did not know how to guide her, and did not require her to renounce useless friendships and fruitless conversations. She had recourse to many other priests, and she summed up her experience by saying that it was better that they should have no knowledge at all than that they should be dabblers. " These confessors," she writes, " certainly did not mean to deceive me, but they knew no better: their decisions left me at even greater liberty. They saw no stumbling block in venial sin. This did great harm to my advancement in virtue, and I think it my duty to say so here, in order that souls may be preserved from such great evil. The first to lead me astray on certain points was a very learned Religious of the Order of St. Dominic." The saint returned often to this subject, and even went so far as to say that a soul ought to remain without a director until such time as it meets with one who has the required dispositions. St. Francis de Sales spoke in the same strain to Philothee: " Choose your confessor from a thousand, said Avila; but for my part, I shall choose him from ten thousand, because it is incredible how few are capable of this office." This advice of the holy Doctor must not be taken too literally, but it certainly is true that a very virtuous confessor, who supplements his practical experience with a knowledge of the means of attaining to perfection, is not often met with.

St. John of the Cross is in complete agreement with St. Francis de Sales and St. Teresa in this matter. The reflections occasioned, in his Commentary on the last strophe of the " Living Flame of Love," by the thought of the prejudice caused to soul through an incompetent confessor, content with an honest mediocrity and uncon- sciously forming souls to it, are of a nature to inspire salutary fear in directors. The great Mystical Doctor, after having shown that the search for a consolation, an acquaintance, a satisfaction, is sufficient to retard a soul's progress, goes on to say; " What terrible damage is thus caused, a matter for regret and pity. . . . A nothing cripples holy inspirations, and the ruin which results for the privileged soul is more lamentable than the faults which cause many less privileged souls to fall." Evidently it will be a Providential favour if, in such a case, a pious or learned director is met with who discerns the apparently trivial obstacle, knows the harm it is doing, and denounces it sweetly but firmly. But, according to St. John of the Cross, a spiritual master is scarcely to be found who knows how to guide souls whom God has begun to introduce to the unitive life. " When God," he writes, " inspires a soul to keep itself quiet and solitary, along comes the spiritual master. He knows only one thing—to be up and doing, and hammering like a blacksmith. Look alive, he says, give over these practices, which are pure laziness, waste of time, illuminism, and foolishness. . . . Spiritual masters who act in this manner, have no idea of recollection or of the spiritual solitude of the soul."

Such considerations, however, ought in no way to discourage souls who are devoted to as perfect a practice as possible of the Christian virtues, counsels, and gifts of the Holy Spirit. Very pious people living in the world may have a wide choice in selecting the confessor who suits them; but this choice must be made in all sincerity, and in prayerfully following the divine inspiration, because many will choose the director who is most sympathetic to them, rather than the director who will point out their faults.

A more frequent case, perhaps, is the following. A soul full of good desires, and having already made progress under an enlightened and virtuous priest, finds itself unable to obey when this priest points out a fault of which the soul itself is ignorant. Self-questioning begins; it seems evident that the confessor is deceived, and the soul refuses to believe or to submit without understanding.

St. John of the Cross has written on this matter. In the way of perfection, there is ordinarily a very painful step to take, in which a person who wishes to attain to union must allow himself to be guided with the docility of a blind man, and, so to speak, with both eyes closed. "From this it follows," he says, "that the person who wishes to unite himself with God must pass through an annihilation of all natural light into the darkness of the obscure night. And this obscurity must remain as long as there are any vestiges of inveterate habits, which have given, in its depths, a wrong tone to the soul."

Religious, especially cloistered Religious, have undoubtedly less freedom than persons in the world in their choice of a director whom they can consult with sufficient frequency, in spite of the liberty accorded to them by recent decrees of Canon Law. But they have the immense advantage of having contracted vows which bind them to the observation of constitutions approved by the Church and suited to the aptitudes and needs of their souls. In default of sustained direction, it will certainly suffice that they follow conscientiously, with the grace of God, the various points of their Rule in order to attain to sanctity, as a great Pope has clearly declared.

The reader will have divined the answer to the question we pose: Why are many called and few chosen? Pious souls, to whom we here address ourselves, do not reach a high habitual state of union because they are lacking in generosity, because they neglect to examine themselves in all sincerity before God, and because they do not respond to all the invitations of grace. St. Thérèse of the Infant Jesus declared: "From the age of three, I refused nothing to the Good God." If many souls were thus faithful, there would be many saints. We hasten to add that if a soul, even after grave sin, makes a resolution to be attentive in future, distrusting self and relying on divine grace, submitting obediently and strictly to all the directives of the Holy Spirit enjoined by its Rule, by its superiors, by its confessor, it will succeed in conforming, habitually and in all things, its will to the will of God. It is usual to cite in this context the case of St. Teresa of Avila. She had vegetated till the age of forty in religious mediocrity, and it was only when she had sacrificed her least attachments that she really entered on the way of holiness, and, having reformed herself, went on to reform also the Carmelite Order. To many of her confessors, the last bond holding her was of no importance and could be ignored; but it was, according to the celebrated comparison of St. John of the Cross, like a thread of silk which binds the bird to earth and prevents it from flying toward the heights.

" One sacrifice above all cost me most," she writes, " the renouncing of certain friendships, *very innocent in themselves*, but to which I was too much attached. It seemed to me, moreover, that I could not break them off without showing ingratitude; so I said to my confessor that, since these relations were innocent in the sight of God, I did not see why I should appear ungrateful." At this stage, though favoured with special graces, St. Teresa was still in that state of mind in which the penitent reasons with the confessor instead of blindly obeying him. Père Balthazar Alvarez, convinced that he was powerless to persuade her, even with the very best of reasons, advised her to recommend the whole matter to God for a few days and to recite the *Veni Creator* in prayer for light. It was then that Jesus spoke to her: " I do not desire that your conversation should be with men, but only with angels."

From this example, it is clear that an apparently trivial obstacle can prevent a Religious or a pious person from becoming a saint and fulfilling his entire mission. If the matter is only cursorily examined, it is easy to suppose that pious souls who failed to attain to a state of eminent union with God and of perfection, had not received graces calling them to such heights; but a closer and more attentive study of their lives will cause us to realize that they have been lacking in generosity, by not renouncing a habit which bound their hearts to earth, and by failing in total self-abnegation. "Never does the Lord refuse us His assistance," says St. Teresa; "the failure and the lack of fidelity is always on our side."

We have established that failure to reach holiness by souls who have sufficient spiritual means and are called by God to a religious or holy life is due to their own infidelity and lack of correspondence with grace. It remains to consider what are the principal imperfections or faults which most frequently retard the soul's progress, and keep it in a state of mediocrity.

We shall not speak of grave faults which the beginner will have corrected in the purgative way. We speak of retarding obstacles, and these we reduce, principally, to three.

We list, first of all, particular friendships. By this, we do not mean culpable relations, but, as St. Teresa said, "certain friendships, innocent in themselves, but to which we give ourselves immoderately." Many souls are crippled by so-called spiritual friendships, which, being always somewhat excessive and exclusive, are too human. One frequently meets with souls who can never deprive themselves of such affections. They spend their whole lives seeking such attachments, so that one attachment succeeds the other, and a whole life, even devout and religious, is spent without attaining to true liberty of spirit and full union with God.

The friendship of which we speak here, is not limited to two people, but it can be found in Communities among a small group of Religious. It brings fatally in its train preferences, sympathies, on the one hand, and dislikes and antipathies, on the other. By the very fact that a person is drawn to esteem, to praise, to value certain people who please him, and to pass over in silence those to whom he is indifferent, he is already guilty of injustice. This partiality, which consists only in always being silent about the qualities of certain people, is not compatible with holiness. This is frequently so with the affection which one bears to a director—an affection which is legitimate in itself, but which can give rise to too many and too prolonged conversations. An affectionate complacency is thus grafted on spiritual friendships and produces effects which are too natural. At the very least, precious time is lost which could be given to God, certain relaxations in silence and some slight failures in the Rule are permitted oneself, which will be a source of disedification to the neighbour. This is not conducive to sanctification or to holiness.

We pass on to the second obstacle to progress in holiness, which arises immediately from the fact that particular friendships among several people occasion party-spirit, self-seeking, ambition, mutual flattery, and can be a very grave obstacle to progress. St. John of the Cross, who had laboured as much and more than anyone else for the reform of the Discalced Carmelites, saw a powerful party growing little by little with particular friendship as its bond, and he denounced with courageous frankness the many inconveniences which resulted from it. " He said that ambition in a Religious was almost incurable,

because it is the most insidious of all. It colours and trans-
forms actions and the manner of acting in such fashion
that it simulates virtue and a superior perfection, so that
even the most learned confessors fail to recognize it for
what it really is." In the least communities, apparently
justified ambitions and, especially, calculated complacen-
cies are indulged in, as though there was a custom
obliging them. " Ah," says Soeur Thérèse, " what poison-
ous praise is offered daily to those who hold the first
places." And this observation, we regret to say, is one
which reflects on superiors and subjects. Now, in the
kingdom of those who sincerely tend to holiness, and make
no concessions to human passion, there are no ambitious
and haughty masters who rule in anger and fear; nor
are there subjects who angle for the favours of those in
authority by excessive deference, by clever condescensions
and by adroitly placed praise. All these are inspired by
natural cleverness, and have in them too much of the spirit
of the world and too little of the spirit of Christ. The saint
and the true disciple of Our Saviour, so far from aspiring
to positions of authority; so far from desiring power, the
esteem of men, notoriety, honours, seeks only to obey, to
be the last of all, to be unknown and forgotten.

Finally, we pass to the third obstacle, not less important
than the preceding two, because it especially affects the
most generous among pious souls. We speak of the
incoercible desire to be ever up and doing. How many,
indeed, who have an unshakable faith and a real love for
God and the neighbour, fail to become saints because
they are too active, and refuse to moderate this activity or
even temporarily desist from it altogether. Bossuet, in
his *Méditations sur l'Évangile*, has eloquently expressed the
absolute necessity for moderation in activity: " How much
there is to prune in thee, O Christian! Would you bear

abundant fruit? Then you must prune that superfluous wood, the wood that pushes itself forward; if you think you must always act, and always be on the outside, you will become too exterior. . . . In the Spring, when the vine begins to grow, it must be cut even to the flower, if its growth is excessive. Cut, heavenly Vinetender, and thou, O Christian soul, do you also cut." To prune in oneself branches which are covered with blossom and which promise abundant fruits of salvation, in order, precisely, to attain to a superabundance of interior life, is the sacrifice which appears hardest and to which even privileged souls, to whom it has been given to conquer all the attachments of the purgative life, find it hard to be resigned. Yet, this is an absolutely necessary condition of holiness.

The amount of pruning which one must do in the matter of superfluous activities is greater than is ordinarily supposed. A pious person who, having mastered all his passions, truly seeks self-sanctification, ought not only to prune activities which, however fruitful of temporal good, have become too many; but he must also refrain from reading too much, even of treatises on the Spiritual Life, and he must also avoid a multiplicity of devotions, however legitimate. We must be careful not to fall into the error of thinking that the soul can be sanctified merely through a number of vocal prayers recited or of penances performed. All experienced directors have met with excellent souls who imagine that they make no progress, that they do not correspond to the Divine Will, when they do not cause great trouble to themselves and when they are not up and doing. St. John of the Cross did not fail to stress, as one of the foundation truths of his doctrine, that even in prayer, after long practice and at the call of God, one should know how to silence the activities of imagination, of reflections, of interior colloquies. This is, above all, what active souls fail to understand and which they find most difficult in practice. They will admit, if put to it, that it is necessary to guard against giving oneself excessively to exterior works, but they will not admit that, in certain cases, it is necessary even to cease from meditation, to cease from interior colloquies and conceptions. But if one takes the view-point that the intimate union of the soul with Our Lord, with the Holy Spirit, with the Father, with the Holy Trinity, requires on our side a wholly passive docility, in which, at least for some instants, all personal activity is suspended and then it becomes clear that to produce words, reflections, conceptions is to act in a too natural manner and, to use St. John's comparison, it is to play the jeweller, the coiner, the blacksmith—in other words, and in the last analysis, one manufactures.

There is, indeed, an infinite difference between what God, in the state of union, inspires and realizes in a soul, and what that soul can realize by its own efforts, even as aided by grace. The thoughts and reflections of an inspired theologian or of a soul which meditates, have, of course, a very great value and are incontestably superior to all exterior works; but compared with the operations of God in the soul which remains passive, they are of a very inferior order and seem of little value.

And thus, in the end, we return to the words which St. John, in the Apocalypse, hears from Christ: " Behold I stand at the door and knock: if any man hear my voice and open to me the door, I shall go in to him, and I shall sup with him, and he with me." When pious souls have conquered all their attachments by ascetic exercises, when they have sufficiently practised discursive medita-tion, it is then that Our Saviour stands at their door, knocking frequently and desiring to be admitted. And it is then, also, that the soul should know how to hold itself in calm and to silence all its noise, of what kind soever. The call of Jesus, the Divine Spouse, though persistent, is ordinarily a whisper which the least noise in the soul can drown, in such wise that the whisper is not heard behind the door.

The powers and faculties of the soul keep up, as it were, a constant babble of talk in our interior house, and therefore their operation must be suspended that silence may hang its veils about us and we may hear. Then, in the absolute silence we hear, through an intimate sense of the soul quickened by divine grace, the sweet call of the Divine Guest who continually knocks. But, as the Beloved Disciple warns us, the soul, by a diligent act of love and a complete gift of self, must open its door fully to the Divine Friend. In the *Canticle of Canticles*, the loved one delayed to answer the knocking, and the Spouse passed by, but only to return very soon. The soul should be prompt in answering that knock by an act of love.

We shall not enter into the details of spiritual betrothal and spiritual marriage, because our aim is merely to introduce the pious soul to the vestibule of holiness. When the soul has attained to complete purity, to recollection, to passivity, and to love, it only remains for it to give complete freedom to the action of the Holy Spirit in its depths. But, we repeat, how difficult it is for directors to persuade fervent and naturally active souls that they must know the moment, in prayer, when they must stop, hold themselves immovable in interior silence, and listen in order that they may give themselves to pure Love.

We add one final and important remark. Vocal prayers, which do not require explicit attention to the words used, are less opposed, in the case of advanced souls, to the state of union than is discursive meditation. The same can be said of an external work, more or less mechanical, which rightly pertains to Martha, but which, not being pressing or troublesome, will not disturb the soul and prevent it from Mary's life of union and contemplation.

That the majority of fervent souls may be led to this degree of self-possession and of recollection in external works, nothing less is required than many choice graces and years given over to different ascetic exercises. Tauler says: " A soul will never know true peace, before it has attained its fortieth year. . . . A man must still wait ten years before the Holy Spirit is given to him, in truth, the Consoler Who will teach him all things." Tauler's " forty years " is evidently a metaphorical or symbolical expression. It would be quite easy to list many saints who scaled the summits of perfection in a much shorter time. Because their span of life was short, these privileged and more generous souls have in a short space fulfilled a long time. On the contrary, one could also cite a much longer list of pious and well-intentioned people who have spent half a century without attaining to perfection or to an habitual state of union with God. Good desires are not lacking to these souls, but they recoil before sacrifices which are necessary but hard on human nature; they have circled in the great circle of the Christian life—the circle of the honest and the ordinary—without ever scaling the heights, thus underlining the truth that many are called but few are chosen.

CONCLUSION

Few are chosen, says Our Lord. We have shown that, at least as regards the perfect, these words are to be understood literally, and we have given the main reasons for this. We must, of course, take cognizance of factors which are beyond human control. How many in the world have not been initiated in the Christian religion, how many are lacking in intelligence or in elementary good sense, how many have physical and moral hereditary blemishes which cannot be cured or corrected; but, in the case of many normally gifted and favoured people of good Christian upbringing, personal responsibility cannot be denied. If any doubts remain, the words of St. John of the Cross should dispel them:

" We must explain here why there are so few who attain to this high state of perfection and of union with God. It is not certain that God wills this grace for a small number of superior souls, since He desires that the heights of perfection should be common to all, but he sends small trials to souls and they show themselves feeble. . . . Then, since God does not find these souls strong and faithful in small trials, He refrains from sending those great trials which are necessary to their sanctification. They are as vessels which serve no purpose. A soul desires to be perfect, but will not allow itself to be led along the way of trials which make the perfect." (*Living Flame of Love*.)

This is a résumé of that Christian goodness and virtuous

mediocrity in which a great number of souls live and die, when they could certainly have done better and have attained even to sanctity. Let us have no doubts on the matter; in spite of our apostolate, in spite of a multitude of retreats and eloquent sermons, in spite of spiritual books read with interest, elect souls, souls who attain to the state of divine union, will always be very few. Sometimes, and perhaps this is even a good thing, preachers, confessors and spiritual writers are, by their generosity, under an illusion in this matter. They hope that, through their exhortations, through the learned treatises and the pleasing literature they compose, by the systems and the reputedly easy way they put forward, the number of souls who detach themselves from all things and unite themselves constantly to Jesus Christ, will grow very great.

In past centuries, the Fathers and a huge host of inspired Doctors and theologians have done more by their writings, their apostolate, and their example, for the sanctification of souls than we could ever but it is necessary that many apostles and disc Christ should take endless trouble in order tha number of souls, now and then, here and the attain to sanctity.

We ordinarily attach too little imp nce to superior souls, because we are more impressed by numbers than by quality. Nevertheless, in every order of things, quantity tends to ensure the emergence of one or more individuals of highest quality. Grace does not destroy nature it has often been said; and that is why the Providence of God, respecting in general the laws of nature, permits a great number of good but mediocre Christians, in order that some souls of great religious genius and of tremendous sanctity may emerge. If we may be permitted a defective comparison, it is as though a great many men should work together to build a sort of human pyramid, of which the meaning is the translucent individuality of its summit. But, in the Christian Church and according to the doctrine of Christ, the greatest of all—bishop, eminent Doctor, heroic saint—puts all his intelligence and all his powers at the service of those who are inferior to him in rank, in mind or in virtue: so that, in a sense, the apex of the pyramid is the servant of its base. It is for this reason that the Sovereign Pontiff, by divine right head of all Christians, styles himself *Servus Servorum Dei*. In doing so, he merely conforms to the teaching of the Gospel: " But he that is first among you, let him be your servant." The same can be said, in their measure, of the founders of Orders and of the saints. They looked on themselves as the humble servants of their brethren.

In fact, and from the historical point of view, the saints, by comparison with the number of pious persons, are the exception and are as rare as the summits in moun-tain chains. How many Christians of the second order must have gone to the making of a Soeur Thérèse of the Infant Jesus. A saint may, at first sight, appear to hold his title to sanctity by reason of his own exclusive efforts. Yet, it has been very well said that a saint is the crowning reward of a virtuous family, and that was certainly the case with St. Thérèse. Moreover, the Religious who knew Soeur Thérèse and her milieu best, spoke of how they believed that the prayers, the abnegation, the teaching and the example of Mère Genevieve, one of the spiritual foundresses of Lisieux, had obtained for the foundation the grace for which she longed, the grace of the gift of a saint to the new Carmel.

It is thus, that, in seeking the roots of the tree on the summit of which we admire an incomparable flower of holiness, one finds elements of varying spiritual value, united and contributing to produce, with the aid of grace, a beautiful ripening of exceptional holiness.

Looked at in this way, holiness, such as we have defined it in the preceding chapters, is, it will be readily understood, extremely exceptional; but we must now underline that, if the saint is in some fashion a result of the virtuous actions which nameless individuals of the Christian community have practised, inversely it is thanks to the action, the heroism, the exceptional merits of certain great apostles and saints, that the commonality of men are Christian and practise, even modestly, the precepts and the virtues recommended by Christ. We would all be pagans had not the disciples of Christ taught us the doctrine and the spirit of the Gospel, often at the cost of their lives. We have taken a glance at Soeur Thérèse and have seen how her holiness was partly due to a number of unknown factors. But, on the other hand, how many of the once indifferent and the unbelieving owe their faith to the little Soeur Thérèse. When a saint comes, he saves an incalculable number of men.

Sodom would have been spared by God had seven just men been found in it. To-day, in our great towns, many baptized persons are found who are just as guilty, but one saintly and perfect soul who walks among them saves a multitude of others by its mission of redemption. If we are ignorant of the number of humble efforts that was required for many Christians to merit the coming of a great saint, we are equally unable to number those who owe their return to faith, their progress in perfection, to the example, the teaching, and the intercession of a humble soul who secretly offers itself as a victim for its fellow men and thus renews or continues the mission of Christ.

The consequences which we can draw from this incontestable truth are very consoling. Notice, first of all, that we have not even thought of listing, among the things that can hinder our sanctification, sins, and even very grave vices, which one has confessed and corrected in a sincere conversion. All theologians agree that, so far from being a hindrance to perfect charity, they can be, on the contrary, the occasion of a greater humility, of a more profound gratitude to the Divine Mercy, and therefore of a more fervent love of God. Moreover, the Gospel and the History of the Church abound in examples of great sinners who became great saints. " To whom much is forgiven," says Christ, " he loveth more; he to whom less is forgiven loveth less." And that is why the Liturgy calls original sin a happy fault—*felix culpa*. When treating of the infinite mercy of God, one must not exclude sinners who have fallen again and again into the gravest sins, but who have repented sincerely and returned with all their heart. All agree that, had Judas prostrated himself at the foot of the Cross, he would have received the same mercy as did the Good Thief. Thus, then, repeated falls into the most grievous sins do not prevent—on the contrary, indeed—great sinners, apostates and sacrilegious men, who submit their whole heart and will in repentance to God, from becoming great saints. " When my son abandon my kingdom," said Christ to St. Angela of Foligno, " they become children of the devil. But if they return to the Father, the joy of the Father is great, and He fills their hearts with superior joy. Such is the Father's joy, that He fills their souls with a joy which even faithful virgins have not tasted. This joy arises from the immense love which the Father bears them, and also from the fact the sinner, knowing the majesty and the clemency of the Lord, recognizes that he is worthy of Hell. That is why, the deeper a man shall have been in the abyss of sin, the deeper may he also be in the abyss of sanctity."

Another consequence which we can draw from the preceding considerations is that, if during our whole life we have practised only moderate virtue, nevertheless, provided we have been careful to avoid grave sin and to live in a state of grace, we have not ceased to be loved by God, to merit Heaven, and to contribute modestly—if only in being, as it were, the stones of the pedestal—to the coming of a great saint. " Though Religious Orders should become relaxed," said Our Lord to St. Teresa of Avila," it would be a mistake to think that they now gave little glory and small service; for what would become of the world if there were no Religious." There are, indeed, Religious observing a mitigated Rule, and straightforward ecclesiastics, who have been employed by God as modest instruments to aid Thérèse de Ahumada to rise aloft and to become one of the lights of the Church.

In conclusion, we return to a truth which we have already enunciated and which is too often forgotten. The Latin authors repeat: *Humanum pancis vivit genus.* Just reserves can be made to this adage. From a natural and, especially, from a supernatural point of view, men live in dependence on the light and the merits of great souls who, as intermediaries, communicate to them spiritual light and spiritual graces; for such is the order required by Providence and by the dogma of the Communion of Saints. Do not the theologians maintain, with good reason, that all the favours given to mortals pass first through the hands of Mary, Mediatrix of Grace. The sculptor of the statue of Soeur Thérèse in Lisieux, has shown her as receiving rose-petals from the hand of the Blessed Virgin and casting them on the whole world. It is a happy and a very just symbol, but perhaps it is also incomplete: for Soeur Thérèse, wishing to associate her daughters and followers on earth with her apostolate, would surely communicate the divine favours to souls by their mediation. There are complex and unsuspected relations in the Communion of Saints, at which we could scarcely guess and about which we could but stammer inadequacies.

If we take the vantage point of efficacious grace and of divine predestination, we ought to be very happy, in spite of grave sins and infidelities, because of the place which it has pleased God to assign to us in the constellation of souls forming the hierarchy of the elect. On our bed of agony we can recognize our unworthiness, yet die in entire confidence of the mercy of the Saviour. It is in this sense that we can give up our soul, in murmuring the words of Scripture: " All things contribute to the good of those who, having been called to salvation, love God "; or again: " Say unto the just that all is good."